One Thing

Insight from top business executives
on what it takes to be a great leader.

Tim Malloy
Billy Martin

Published by X60 Media, LLC

OneThingTheBook.com

Graphics by Tony Saura,
Saura Design, Marlton NJ

FIRST EDITION
ISBN: 9781081145484

For updates, additional resources, and bulk orders visit:
OneThingTheBook.com

*To my wife, Pattie, whose unconditional love and constant support in
the ebb and flow of our medical challenges together
have made all of the difference.*

*To my children, Matthew and Mary Frances, I pray that I have been a
good example of how to be a loving and considerate spouse and partner;
a nurturing and instructive parent;
and an ethical and resilient business person.*

*And to my grandchildren, Alana and Jameson, I encourage you to focus
on deciding the type of person you want to be. If you do, the question
of, 'what do I want to do' will be easier to answer.*

-- Tim

*To Norma Jean, you are an inspiration every day on how the
underdog can always grab the golden ring.*

*To my five girls -- Jenn, Jess, Alissa, Vicky, and Claudia – find your
"one thing" in life and reach for the stars. You all are truly amazing!*

*And to Beth – your belief in my creative side fuels everything I do.
Thank you for the support and encouragement for the
past ten years and beyond.*

-- Billy

We would like to thank all of the executive contributors who shared their time and talent to make this book possible.

Your experience, insight and generous spirit will provide a meaningful boost to aspiring leaders and sales professionals who make the decision to incorporate this collection of "ONE THING" strategies into their daily business practices.

We also want to recognize and thank our extended family and friends whose words and deeds have set a standard of excellence that have inspired us to follow your path to personal and professional fulfillment.

-Tim and Billy

One Thing Content

Introduction

In a memorable scene from the hit movie, City Slickers, the crusty old cowboy Curly Washburn offers a bit of sage advice to Billy Crystal's character, Mitch Robbins, on the secret of life being just one thing.

Curley reveals to Mitch, what we all come to learn in time, is that the elusive 'one thing' is something uniquely different for all of us. And so it becomes an individual challenge to discover the one thing that will be the catalyst for positive change and help us widen the path to achieve personal fulfillment and professional success.

Now, there were no cowboys consulted in the writing of this book. However, we did seek out the wisdom of dozens of successful business executives and respected thought leaders.

It's a collection of (one) things that are guaranteed to help you be successful.

And we asked them to reflect and share just one thing aspiring sales leaders and professionals can follow and incorporate into your daily business life. The answers we received were as varied as they were insightful.

They do serve as a valuable compass to assist you in perhaps finding or confirming your ordained path, then propelling you on it, and keeping you from straying off it. The dynamic men and women interviewed for this book typically offered a couple of one thing topics for consideration, but when they were closely evaluated under the light of, 'if you could tell an aspiring sales professional just one thing that you wish you had known earlier, what would it be,' their choice became more clear.

If you come away from reading this book embracing but a single one thing, then our efforts and your time will have been well spent. But we are confident there will be several 'one things' offered on these pages that will introduce or reinforce a practice that will elevate your leadership skills.

There is indeed power in a single element of change that you are about to consider. The research of Malcolm Gladwell (*The Tipping Point*) and Edward Lorenz (*The Butterfly Effect*) dramatically underscores this position.

So whether you read it cover to cover, or scan the Table of Contents for the names or topics that intrigue you, this book will provide numerous one things that have the potential to make you a more valuable leader and a more valued person in your business world.

Thank you for your support and good luck on your journey!

Tim Malloy

About the Author: Tim Malloy

A passion for all facets of business relationships earned Tim success and high praise in careers in sports marketing, corporate sales and as an entrepreneur.

Tim was the Assistant Group Sales Director and Public Relations Director for the Philadelphia 76ers before working as an award-winning Sales and Promotions Representative for Converse Inc. He holds a U.S. Patent on a golf training glove that received a 4-star rating in Golf magazine and is a former college basketball official.

These accomplishments came in healthy stretches of a lifelong battle with Neurofibromatosis that has required 32 surgeries to date while struggling at times to breathe, speak, and swallow.

Tim pushed forward and shifted his professional focus to writing and has co-authored five books in the area of sports officiating.

With a strong desire to give thanks for his Blessings, Tim is the co-founder of The Zebra Foundation, a nonprofit organization that underwrites the cost of training and outfitting military and law enforcement personnel to be sports officials.

Tim is a graduate of St. Joseph's University and resides in West Deptford, NJ with his wife, Pattie. They love and enjoy the company of their children, Matthew and Mary Frances, and their grandchildren, Alana and Jameson.

LinkedIn.com/in/refwriter

Prologue:
What is Leadership?

We all play a leadership role at one time or another.

On any given day, a Google or Amazon search on the topic of "sales leadership" will literally put hundreds of millions of informative links and thousands of book titles at your disposal, respectively.

Whether you are holding the formal managerial reins -- or you are an individual contributor responsible for generating sales (and revenue) leveraging an extended team of resources -- we all assume a leadership position with the people who follow us.

Leaders help people focus on achieving goals and removing obstacles.

Spending a majority of the past ten years at cloud computing giant Salesforce (NYSE: CRM), and studying the habits of great (and not so great) leaders, some interesting dynamics were surfaced.

Here's a few of the key findings.

1) Great leaders ARE "force multipliers." It's all about taking the native talent surrounding you and getting the most of their time and talents. Regardless whether you lead a formal team or coordinate the efforts of various resources, being a multiplier is a key focus.

All of the ideas in this book are force multiplying in nature. Implementing small changes in your work-style or lifestyle may produce exponential gains in productivity.

2) Teams want to be coached -- NOT managed. When team members are asked the question --- "what's the **'one thing'** my leader can do to get more performance out of me?" The answer is always the same, *"Give me more coaching!"* Not, help me manage my business; not, help me close more deals; not, help me gain more knowledge. It's all about coaching them more closely.

Contained in the following chapters are dozens of tactical coaching tips and tactical advice to focus on being a better coach, and less of a burdensome manager.

3) Some business practices that look good in theory can actually detract from your team or company performance. These "self-diminishing" tactics which are based on sound principles of business logic can cause our team members to be less effective and reduce our capacity to deliver results.

Undoubtedly, deciding where to put your time and treasure to improve your coaching ability can be a daunting and tedious task. Like examining a large container of collected coins, you want to quickly separate the rare from the common and focus on the items of value that can make a difference in your world.

We believe with the material contained between the covers of this book will give you a huge head start on identifying the valuable leadership currency that will move you faster and further along your career path -- or be the catalyst to plot a new course.

But make no mistake, if you are in the business of driving sales performance and you rely on other people to achieve that goal --- you ARE a leader.

Billy Martin

About the Author: Billy Martin

Billy Martin is currently a Senior Director for Strategic Programs and Leadership Development at Medidata Solutions. (NASDAQ:MDSO)

After spending ten years at cloud computing giant, Salesforce.com (NYSE: CRM) he works with the industry's brightest stars to help them be better leaders and dynamic coaches to drive sales performance.

Billy has a Masters Degree in Sports Medicine (MEd) and taught Anatomy, Physiology and Biology at both the secondary school and collegiate level. He transitioned into the business world after receiving an MBA degree in Technology Management. While spending several years in the medical sales arena with Smith+Nephew he eventually co-founded several technology companies on his journey toward leadership development.

In addition to the passion for writing (six Amazon.com Top Sellers) he loves teaching sports officiating --- and does so for high school soccer and basketball, as well as collegiate softball. You can find these teachings at Ref60.com the world's leading educational website for basketball officials.

Billy is passionate about leadership development and has co-launched a program specifically designed to drive coaching for sales performance (FLIPDCoaching.com).

Living in Wildwood, NJ he enjoys family, friends and time on the water chasing that elusive Striped Bass.

LinkedIn.com/in/crmbilly/

1

"Be more introspective."

Dan Hilferty
CEO, Independence Health Group

The noted Swiss psychiatrist, Carl Jung believed that our visions only become clear to us when we dare to look inside of our heart. The father of analytical psychology succinctly stated that *'who looks outside, dreams; who looks inside, awakes.'*

Now deep introspection will help to reveal the true path you are meant to travel, but deciding to take this clarified journey can create its own challenges. Age and personal obligations can narrow the road of self-discovery and seem to tilt it all uphill.

Focus on doing good while doing well.

But ultimately, it's the blending of spirit and skill that answers the life-fulfilling question of what endeavor you should passionately pursue that will allow you to make the living you desire while positively impacting others.

First, determine if you are on the right path or whether you are being called to chart a new course. From this direction-setting deep dive, your journey will now be fueled by the personal mandate of, *'doing good while doing well.'* Once this is determined you will begin to observe signs that success can be more easily arrived at when you are willing to take a leadership position for a common cause or be a valued and complementary part of a shared vision or goal.

Success will come into view at the realization that you are part of a collaborative team and it will grow in abundance when each member agrees to make a selfless contribution to a greater good.

Introspective leaders understand the strengths and gifts, as well as the weaknesses and blind spots of their staff. Introspective leaders also carefully assemble their teams to maximize individual performances with the goal of achieving something greater than themselves.

Project Aristotle, a two-year research study of almost 200 teams at Google revealed that the essential ingredients of successful group collaborations are rooted in the members feeling respected and having their work valued. The study also concluded team members:

- Want to feel their work is playing an important part in the company's overall success.
- Need to feel a high level of personal satisfaction from the work they perform daily.
- Need to know their suggestions will be given careful consideration and not dismissed out of hand. Good people can have honest disagreements.
- Thrive on the assurances of being able to depend on their teammates.
- Maximize their efforts when they are clear on their role and where their contribution fits into the success of the project.

However, before you can lead a successful group or be a vital and valued part of an image-of-difference team, you must **do the important introspective work** to understand what you are called to do and where you are being called to do it. Here are some ideas how:

Quiet on the Set!
Find a consistent time and place to be uninterrupted and alone with your thoughts.

Can I Ask Myself a Question?
Whether it is sitting quietly or taking a secluded walk, several deep breaths will clear your mind to explore the WHAT, WHY and HOW questions of your life.

When you allow your mind to flow with the currents of your spirit, you begin to be your most authentic self and make your most valuable contributions to others.

This is the optimum personal state of clarity that transforms people into leaders who can galvanize a group around a detailed mission and motivates individuals to proudly submit their best efforts for a worthy objective.

Leaders and workers flourish in settings that allow for seamless collaboration.

Here are some other ways to create these settings of success:

Paint a Passionate Picture of Purpose
Write down in great detail the goal you want the team to rally around, and the measurable action steps to get there.

Build on Strengths
A great bonding exercise is to administer a personality test (i.e., True Colors or DISC) and share the results in a group setting. This view of vulnerability creates a deeper commitment within the team and allows the leader to accent each member's strengths and minimize their shortcomings.

Encourage Outside the Box Thinking
Energize the group atmosphere with constant creative thinking and regular brainstorming sessions. An inquisitive mindset is the death knell for pesky problems.

Celebrate Those Who Collaborate
No one has ever died of an overdose of appreciation, and the best way to produce more rewarding collaborative behavior is to recognize it.

So, curtail looking outward and dreaming of what might be, and begin to search deep within to awaken greatness in you that will have you poised to collaborate with others and deliver personal and team success!

About Dan Hilferty

Dan is the CEO of Independence Health Group, parent of Independence Blue Cross, one of the nation's leading health insurers.

Since Dan became CEO in 2010, the company has tripled in size, expanding through its affiliates to 27 states and the District of Columbia, and serving 8.2 million people nationwide.

As a sought-after speaker on leadership, transforming health care, including the role of technology and big data, Mr. Hilferty has appeared on MSNBC, Fox Business Network, CNN, and in *The New York Times*, *The Wall Street Journal*, and other national media.

Dan is also the chairman of the board of directors for the Chamber of Commerce for Greater Philadelphia, and he serves on the executive committee of America's Health Insurance Plans. In addition, Mr. Hilferty is a member of the Board of Directors for Aqua America, where he is also the lead independent director, and FS Investment Corporation III. He is the immediate past chairman of the board of directors of the Blue Cross Blue Shield Association, which represents Blue plans covering 106 million Americans. In 2015, he served as co-chair on the executive leadership cabinet of the World Meeting of Families which brought Pope Francis to Philadelphia.

Dan earned his undergraduate degree from St. Joseph's University in Philadelphia, Pennsylvania, and then served in the Jesuit Volunteer Corps running a community center in Portland, Oregon. After earning a master's degree in public administration from American University, he returned to the Philadelphia area where he lives with his wife, Joan. The couple has five children and three grandchildren.

Dan's Recommendations

Read One Book
Pope Francis: Why He Leads, The Way He Leads - Chris Lowney
Learn about the first Jesuit Pope from America's leading Jesuit publisher.

Visit One Website
IBX.com
Independence Blue Cross serves more than 8 million people nationwide and nearly 2.5 million people in the Philadelphia region.

Subscribe to One Podcast
Growing Greater Philadelphia Podcast & Radio
Selectgreaterphl.com/podcast/
Showcases the amazing stories of economic growth in the Philadelphia area, and the people behind them.

2

"Hire people that you can learn from."

Kara Goldin
Founder & CEO, hint Inc.

The industrialist icon, Andrew Carnegie, once suggested his epitaph should read, *"Here lies a man who was able to surround himself with men far cleverer than himself."*

The business magnate's modesty notwithstanding, the message is a timeless and universal one. Seek out the best and the brightest talent for your corporate team and eschew the urgings of your ego to be the smartest person in the room.

Are you prepared to embrace smart people in your business environment?

When you set a standard to hire people who are smarter than yourself, you will discover you are creating an ever-flowing source of knowledge for learning. And you are adding vital members to the corporate team who want to be challenged and inspired, and do not need, or want to be micromanaged.

By securing gifted employees and giving them the freedom to do their job unencumbered you are making a critical contribution to corporate morale. Gallup research indicates nearly 75% of employees voluntarily leave their jobs due to friction with controlling managers. This image-of-difference practice also frees you up to explore new opportunities for growth.

Also, you are also building in a safeguard to prevent limiting the company to the level of your own ability and therefore grow the capabilities of the organization.

And, if it's true in the real estate rental business that, *'a bad tenant is worse than no tenant,'* then the same can be said about a bad employee hire.

Research conducted by the Harvard Business Review reveals:

Bad hiring decisions can account for up to 80% of employee turnover.

This quite often could have been significantly reduced by hiring the smartest and most qualified candidate. Additional studies indicate that turnover costs range between 50% to a staggering 500% of employee annual wages.

But it takes more than a willingness to sublimate your ego to fill your stable with thoughtful thoroughbreds. You must know the right questions to ask in order to assess and evaluate each potential candidate before making the critical decision.

Chart a Smart People Profile

Your hiring radar should be set to identify candidates who are passionate and positive about the business. They emanate a confidence of knowing what is required or how to figure it out independent of your close guidance. And they are active listeners who you could envision seeking out for solutions to problems. They also carry themselves with a 'humble swagger;' confident and self-assured without being arrogant or condescending.

Set Your Talent Code

Establish a tone and tempo that welcomes smart people who have traveled a different, but nevertheless distinguished path, to achieve excellence. This includes knowing the premier talent recruiters who understand your ever-changing marketplace.

Prepare and Perfect Your Process

Respected recruiting firms are great, but your own team will likely have a compelling list of candidates to consider. And when it's time to meet with potential hires, be prepared with several carefully crafted questions and a consistent grading formula. Ideally, these interviews are done in person in order to better observe non-verbal and body language cues.

Candidates with the right stuff generally have a keen sense of self-awareness.

They know their true strengths and genuine weaknesses and can speak candidly about both.

Once you have made the critical decision and the candidate has accepted the offer to join the team, you must set them up for success. That means being detailed in the new employee's role and responsibilities, plus providing the necessary support to stack the odds for success heavily in your favor.

All successful leaders and owners come to realize that their most valuable corporate asset is the human capital holding it all together. And the brighter your people are, the more likely you will be to share the feelings of Mr. Carnegie's corporate epitaph!

About Kara Goldin

Entrepreneur Kara Goldin is the founder and CEO of hint, Inc., a healthy lifestyle brand that produces the leading, award-winning, unsweetened flavored water, as well as a scented sunscreen spray that is oxybenzone and paraben free.

Kara has received numerous accolades, including being named, EY Entrepreneur of the Year 2017 Northern California; one of Fast Company's Most Creative People In Business; Fortune's Most Powerful Women Entrepreneurs; and Forbes' 40 Women To Watch Over 40. The Huffington Post listed her as one of the six disruptors in business, alongside Steve Jobs and Mark Zuckerberg.

Previously, Kara was Vice President of Shopping and E-commerce Partnerships at AOL, where she helped lead the growth of its startup shopping business to a $1 billion enterprise.

Kara is an active business speaker and writer, and, in 2016, she launched the Kara Network, a digital resource and mentoring platform for entrepreneurs. She also recently launched the podcast, Unstoppable, where she interviews founders, entrepreneurs, and disruptors across various industries.

Follow Kara on LinkedIn and on Twitter by visiting drinkhint.com and thekaranetwork.com.

Kara's Recommendations

Read One Book
Blitzscaling by Reid Hoffman
The lightning-fast path to building massively valuable companies.

Visit One Website
DrinkHint.com
"Hint is disrupting the beverage industry." -- The Today Show

Subscribe to One Podcast
"How I Built This" by Guy Raz
Share in the narrative journey about innovators, entrepreneurs, and idealists - and the movements they built.

3

"Embrace the mad customers."

Shawn Vanderhoven
Founder, UP
& Partner at the Wiseman Group

Angry, dissatisfied customers can be viewed as a looming tornado or an active bees' nest – and most people run fast and far in the opposite direction of these seemingly nothing-but-trouble scenarios.

But storm chasers and beekeepers know there is valuable data available and sweet profit to be earned by moving towards these troublesome situations.

Do what others won't do.

Identifying and getting in front of your company's unhappy customers is a winning strategy that leaders and account managers need to build into their repertoire.

Take a step back to plan your move forward

When we widen our view, we can see more clearly that the quickest and surest way to achieve our goals (i.e., increased sales; more compensation; career advancement) is to solve the problems of dissatisfied customers.

These disgruntled clients want to do business with you – they were already in the fold – but left in a huff over a misstep somewhere in the process between a previous order and the execution in delivering it.

Whatever the reason for their angst, they grew frustrated with your company's ability to perform and abandoned your empty promises.

But while the mad customer may have given up on you; do not give up on them!

The mad customer is the big game you want to hunt down. Despite their orneriness and loud roar of disapproval for previous wrongs, their feedback is your company's road to redemption. Exalt the unhappy client and view their unvarnished criticism for what it is – the answer to what needs to change to reignite this relationship.

And setting your sights on steadily mending the broken business bonds with former accounts will also provide a dual benefit of creating a positive customer reference to present to a prospect when your attention is turned to landing new business.

In the middle of difficulty lies opportunity.

So here are a few actions steps to consider when you summon the courage to take on the challenge of flipping mad customers to glad customers:

The Target Market
Follow corporate procedures to identify the accounts you want to revitalize. Scrutinize CRM tools to prioritize former customers who are no longer doing any business, as well as current accounts whose once dominating presence has withered away and are no longer included in any company forecast projections.

The Starfish Philosophy
"I can make a difference with this one!" is what the young boy said in the *'Parable of the Starfish'* as he tossed back one of the thousands of tiny sea creatures that had washed ashore in reply to the old man scoffing at his efforts. Harness that same optimistic spirit and start to make a difference with one mad customer. Through careful research, identify at least one solution you can deliver on from what may be a laundry list of issues.

Rehearse the Resolution Ritual
Like all skills, practice makes perfect, so make role playing a part of your self-improvement regimen. Playing the role of the mad customer can be an enlightening activity and help you become more proficient in mastering the ability to diffuse conflict and avoid taking harsh corporate criticism as a personal attack.

Apologize and Empathize

When it's time to meet with the mad customer bring with you an open mind, a contrite heart, and sharp ears. You can respectfully ask for pardon for the previous corporate missteps, without groveling or bad mouthing those responsible for the decisions and performances that have contributed to the current situation.

Listening with genuine concern and careful note taking will uncover a need, no matter how small, that is fixable and can slow the negative roll and be the watershed moment that jettisons this account off the mad customer list.

So, if you want professional rewards that are satisfying on several levels, embrace a mad customer today!

About Shawn Vanderhoven

Shawn Vanderhoven is a Partner at the Wiseman Group and heads the leadership practice for senior executives and emerging leaders.

He is a collaborator on the Second Edition and New York Times Bestseller, *Multipliers: How the Best Leaders Make Everyone Smarter.*

Shawn consults with companies around the world on how to build an intelligence culture. Shawn has co-designed leadership development strategies with executives at leading brands like, Capital One, Deloitte, Google, Intel, LinkedIn, and Salesforce.

Before working in executive development, Shawn grew his family's software business by 30x. He lives in Menlo Park, California with his wife and three sons, where he is researching the neuroscience behind why we follow certain leaders.

Shawn's Recommendations

Read One Book

Leadership and Self-Deception: Getting Out of the Box
by The Arbinger Institute
An international bestseller that offers its insight on motivation, conflict, and collaboration that can benefit organizations and individuals.

Visit One Website

TheWisemanGroup.com
The Wiseman Group helps you become a leader that accesses potential.

Subscribe to One Podcast

Box of Crayons - The Great Work Podcast – Michael Bungay Stainer
An engaging and practical podcast that provokes you to do less Good Work and more Great Work.

4

"Name and claim your Noble Sales Purpose."

Lisa McLeod
Founder, McLeod and More, Inc.

It is the question that every leader and sales executive needs to ask themselves:

Do you have a Noble Purpose; or do you just sell stuff?

The answer to this critical query is linked directly to your individual success and satisfaction, as well as corporate profitability.

There needs to be a distinct shift away from focusing on hitting quotas and closing deals, to a fresh mindset that concentrates on improving the lives of current customers and finding new ones who could benefit from what you are selling.

Having absolute clarity about how to make a difference with clients, and how to do it differently than your competition is key.

Purpose is the secret to driving more revenue.

The data from over a decade-long study of more than 50,000 brands around the world shows that companies who put improving people's lives at the center of all they do have a growth rate triple that of their competitors and they outperform the market by over 350%.

The research confirms that organizations with a Noble Sales Purpose have a competitive advantage, and the absence of a Noble Purpose creates **three significant problems** for an organization:

Inability to Attract and Retain Top Talent
Money alone is no longer enough. Human beings are hardwired with a need to make a difference. A Noble Sales Purpose

provides a rallying cry and a proven path for success and satisfaction.

Lack of Competitive Differentiation

Offering a solution to the customer's needs, not wedging in features and benefits, is the key to being an image-of-difference organization. Working from a Noble Purpose reframes your customer interactions and diffuses a price war and line-by-line competitive comparisons.

Turf Wars and Silos

In the absence of a Noble Sales Purpose, departmental goals become the default positions, and the natural internal battles begin. A Noble Purpose will act as the North Star and ultimately guide everyone to find the best path to achieve the main organizational goal.

The irony is unavoidable. When you focus on the external goal of improving the lives of your customers instead of the internal target of hitting a quota, you wind up achieving the financial and career success you have desired all along.

A Noble Sales Purpose is not a tactic. It is a strategic shift in the way to approach your business.

Name your Noble Purpose.

The most effective way to craft and polish your own Noble Purpose is to **answer three critical questions:**

Question 1: How Do You Make A Difference?

Think deeply about how what you sell affects the lives of customers. Understand how your performance, and that of your product, impacts their business and day-to-day operations.

Question 2: What Sets You Apart?

Hone in on an accurate assessment of what sets you apart from the competition. Are you better? Are you faster? Do you care more?

Question 3: What Do You Love About Your Job?

Envision your best day on the job and describe what excites you about performing your duties and doing them for your employer.

With these introspective answers in hand you can now create a unique and compelling Noble Purpose narrative that will:

Be True and Be Short

It must be absolutely 100% accurate, and you should be able to tell the story in less than two minutes or 300 words or less.

Describe the Impact on the Customer

A good sales purpose story includes events and consequences. Customers should see who the events affected and the implications for their business.

Include Vivid Details

Action words add energy and drama to the story. Dramatic photos can make it even more powerful.

Strike an Emotional Chord

Shape your Noble Purpose to convey how lives were changed in some fashion.

Support Your Noble Purpose

The story's value is not to entertain clients or potential customers; it is to authenticate your noble sales purpose.

Everyone, on some level, strives for a Noble Purpose and to be a part of something bigger than themselves. Focusing on improving the lives of customers will maximize your abilities and bring forth unparalleled success for you and your company.

About Lisa McLeod

Lisa Earle McLeod is the global expert on purpose-driven sales. Her bestselling book, *Selling with Noble Purpose* introduced Noble Purpose into the business vernacular. Her research reveals why organizations with a purpose bigger than money actually make more money, and they experience greater customer and employee retention.

Lisa, a former Procter & Gamble Sales trainer, now runs her own consulting firm, McLeod & More, Inc. Her firm's clients include Hootsuite, Roche, Volvo, and Dave & Buster's. Lisa is a prolific writer; she is the author of five books and over 2,000 articles. She is the sales leadership expert for Forbes.com and has appeared on the Today show and the NBC Nightly News.

Her newest book, *Leading with Noble Purpose: How to Create a Tribe of True Believers* has been called a breakthrough that is transforming the way leadership is conducted at every level of organizations.

Lisa's Recommendations

Read One Book
The 4 Agreements: A Practical Guide to Personal Freedom
by D.M. Ruiz.
It will improve your leadership skills more than any technique
found in a business book.

Visit One Website
LinkedIn Learning (Linkedin.com/learning/me)
You can learn anything from how to be a purpose-driven seller
or how to play the ukulele.

Subscribe to One Podcast
Work Life from Adam Grant (AdamGrant.net/worklife)
Go inside the minds of some of the world's most unusual
professionals to better work life. The Porsche of Podcasts, per
Inc. Magazine.

5

"Factor in gut instincts when making key decisions."

Rich Miller
CEO (Retired), Virtua Health

Albert Einstein's belief that intuition does not come to an unprepared mind is perhaps the essence of combining art and science when making important business decisions.

The ability to take into your mind the raw, hard data of an important situation facing you on any given day, and then digest it in your gut with experience and instincts, is a powerful two-step process. The top benefit means delivering more favorable outcomes than relying on either separately.

Intuition can contribute speed and experience.

Now whether it is a feeling in the pit of their stomach, or a quiet voice in their head, successful leaders have learned to rely on their instincts because they understand the marketplace rewards innovation, authenticity, and image of difference business decisions.

Research conducted at the University of New South Wales in Australia by psychology professor Joel Pearson defined intuition as the influence of "nonconscious emotional information" from the body or brain, such as an instinctual feeling or sensation. The study showed that information subconsciously perceived in the brain will help with decisions -- provided that information holds some value or extra evidence beyond what people already have in their conscious mind.

There is no shortage of data, numbers, statistics and key performance indicators to be evaluated that can freeze a manager in their tracks. Instinctive skills that are poker-hot can help thaw out the process and get things flowing quickly in the right direction.

Hard data is a not a guaranteed predictor of future outcomes. A leader whose mind and gut are tightly connected may have a more compelling reason to go against the easier and safer decision at hand.

Research conducted at the University of Gottingen in Germany revealed that the human brain functions like a computer only when considering trivial decisions. Complex matters, however, bring into play a process in which knowledge, experience, and emotions are factored into the decision. It has been demonstrated that people who have acquired deep wells of knowledge and experience through their curiosity and a readiness to seize opportunities are able to reach good intuitive decisions more often than those who possess a limited amount of experience.

And the more this sixth sense is exercised and developed, the stronger aide it can be in stacking the decision deck in your favor.

The Sound of Silence
Practice unplugging from the world and allow your mind to be still and quiet. An active, racing mind cannot hear your intuition's soft voice and gentle prodding. Become more proficient at sensing your gut feeling.

Map Out Your Choices
Make a comparative list with data driven information on the left side and intuitive reasoning on the right side. Perform a gap analysis on the potential outcome of each variable.

Get More Gut Checks
Ask colleagues, who have no data to interpret, for their gut feeling on a matter at hand. Provide only enough information to allow them to make a reasonable intuitive choice. Add this info to the choice mapping list above.

The Joy Is In The Journal

Keep a log of all of the times you felt your intuition pointing a specific decision, and note what the results were and whether or not you followed the intuitive choice. The more you pay attention to the consequences of not following your instincts, or note the benefits gained when you did, you will be demonstrably shown how powerful this "sacred gift" (Einstein's description!) is and will become more trusting of it.

Monitor For Emotional Distortion

Look for instances where emotions could be clouding your perception of the situation being evaluated. Call on trusted advisors to assist you in assessing whether personal biases or desires are distorting your instincts.

Molding high levels of industry knowledge with an introspective knowledge of self are the perfect blend of art and science to making wise business decisions.

About Rich Miller

Rich recently retired as president and CEO of Virtua where he served since 1998. Virtua is a non-profit healthcare system offering a full continuum of primary, preventative, wellness, acute and long-term care. Miller led Virtua in innovative directions by creating a values-based culture defined by the "Star Initiative," adopting Six Sigma, and transforming a group of community-based hospitals into technologically advanced regional medical centers.

In addition to an enterprise alliance with GE Healthcare, under Miller's leadership Virtua formed clinical alliances with nationally renowned organizations such as Penn Medicine and The Children's Hospital of Philadelphia (CHOP). Rich has been recognized nationally with appointments to the Leadership Advisory Council of the Joint Commission Center for Transforming Healthcare (CTH) and to the Governing Council of Healthcare Executives for the American Hospital Association.

He is a Fellow of the American College of Healthcare Executives and served as a trustee of the National Quality Forum.

Rich Miller is a sought-after speaker on all facets of business and leadership and can be reached via email- rmbusstrat@gmail.com

Rich's Recommendations

Read One Book
Good To Great by Jim Collins.
Captivating insight on why some companies make the leap...
and others don't.

Visit One Website
Foundation.Virtua.org
You will find stories of hope and inspiration from Virtua
patients, clinicians, donors and community partners who
experience firsthand the power a gift to the Virtua Foundation
can have.

6

"Make time and create moments to be curious."

Fredrik Schuller
Senior Vice President & Partner, BTS

The world-renowned theoretical physicist, Albert Einstein, often stated quite plainly, *"I have no special talents. I am only passionately curious."*

These words, on their face, are absurdly modest since they come from the man who developed one of the two pillars of modern physics and changed the way we look at the universe.

Presumably, Einstein was not intentionally diminishing his intellectual skill set. But likely instead emphasizing the influence his profoundly inquisitive nature had on utilizing his abilities in mathematics and science.

Now few would ever discount the role that brains and talent play in building and creating success in any endeavor. But it is people on all points on the intellectual grid with an insatiable desire to probe the way things are and explore a path for a better way that has fueled all of the medical and technological advancements we enjoy today.

And it is the curiosity 'muscle' that we should exercise vigorously in order to maximize our professional potential.

Why ask why?

Research conducted at the University of California – Davis and the Mayo Clinic revealed that maintaining an active curious mind sharpens and prolongs a person's mental acuity.

Evidence indicates that the human brain retains information better if we are curious about the material. Medical imaging dramatically shows the area of the brain that energizes people to go out and seek rewards looks the same as when we are curious and releases the 'feel good' chemical, dopamine.

While studies demonstrate that people who can remain intellectually active and stimulated throughout their life offer themselves a protective barrier against late-life dementia, it is also the fertile and professionally productive here-and-now that benefits significantly from a curious spirit.

Be Poised For New
When you are curious about something, your mind begins to naturally default to a state of considering new ideas related to the topic. Inquisitiveness will bring forth more creative solutions that will lead to steady success and career growth.

Relationship Builder
Perhaps nothing forges a deeper bond with a colleague or client than showing a genuine interest in the person. Dale Carnegie famously stated, *'you can make more friends in two months by becoming interested in other people than you can in two years trying to get other people interested in you.'*

Everyone has a level of 'perpetual' curiosity – that uneasy feeling that occurs when something surprises you. But what we want to enhance is an 'epistemic' curiosity, which is a pleasurable state associated with anticipation of reward. This is the rocket fuel that drives research and delivers watershed moments.

Consider curiosity as a 'mental itch' that must be scratched and the only way to sooth it is to keep walking through new doors of posed questions and seeing what is on the other side. Sadly, the innate curiosity that everyone is born with is steadily worn down in the interest of conformity. But the good news is this valuable trait can be relearned and strengthened.

First, it is essential to understand there is a difference between being curious and being nosy. At the outset, do not ask too many questions, particularly personal ones. And be sure you are asking with a sincere desire to understand the other person, and not merely because you want the answer.

Pure Listening
Practice listening with no prejudgment. A curious mind listens to gain a more in-depth perspective on the matter at hand to explore alternative best solutions with no investment in a predetermined outcome.

Open-Ended Questions
Initiate questions that provide ample space to collect multifaceted responses. Lead with, "how – what – when – where – why" questions to avoid getting "yes or no" answers.

Be in the Moment
Bring laser focus to every conversation. Distractions and multitasking are curiosity-killers.

Curious Planning
Schedule time to step back and scrutinize fundamental principles guiding your business practices. Doing something just because that is the way it has always been done is not sufficient justification for continuing to do it.

Ask For Advice
Prefacing a question with, *"I would like to get your opinion on…"* in a curiosity moment makes the conversation more authentic and will elevate the depth of the reply.

So perhaps it is true that curiosity has killed more than a few inquisitive cats. But in today's competitive and ever-changing world, the rewards from making a conscious effort to be genuinely curious far outweigh the risks!

About Fredrik Schuller

Fredrik began his career at BTS in 2004 and during his tenure has developed some of BTS' largest customer relationships and pioneered the application of highly customized business simulations for leading Fortune 500 clients such as Chevron, Salesforce.com, NetApp and Autodesk. He focuses on helping senior executives shape and accelerate the execution of transformations and build the leadership to execute on today's business while discovering tomorrow's business.

Fredrik currently runs the West Coast business for BTS and has innovated many of BTS' simulation platforms and execution services in close collaboration with clients.

Prior to BTS, Fredrik received his degree in Management Science/Operations Research from the University of Strathclyde in Glasgow. Fredrik wrote his dissertation on developing a Multi Criteria Decision Analysis framework for public spending. Fredrik was born and raised in Drobak, Norway, has two kids at 1 and 3 years old and enjoys kite surfing and ice hockey in his spare time.

Frederik's Recommendations

Read One Book
Fierce Invalids Home From Hot Climates by Tom Robbins.
It will make you question things more.

Visit One Website
BTS Insights (bts.com/blog)
Explore thought provoking articles from industry leaders on dozens of topics to drive business success.

Subscribe to One Podcast
Revisionist History by Malcolm Gladwell
A journey through the 'overlooked and misunderstood.' Every episode re-examines something from the past and asks if we got it right the first time.

7

"Tell more emotionally engaging personal stories."

Amy Posey
CEO, Peak Teams

People may forget what you said, but they will never forget how you made them feel.

A quick examination of our personal and professional experiences will undoubtedly validate this statement and underscore the art of storytelling as a critical skill in the growth of sales professionals.

The acceptance and value of the ability to tell compelling and emotionally engaging personal stories continue to grow in all sectors of business. Storytelling is becoming a widely-practiced method of delivering corporate messages.

People seem to instinctively resist the notion of bringing their own persona into a business setting when a persuasive case can be made that you are your best self when you bring your total self to work.

Personal stories that are emotionally engaging build better relationships.

When you evoke emotions in others, you make things more memorable from a neuroscience standpoint.

Two parts of the brain that deal with emotion and memory – the hippocampus and the amygdala – are located right next to each other. When you share something that stirs a person emotionally, they will remember it much longer than just a cold statement of fact or the sterile features and benefits of a product.

The need to stifle an urge to "show up and throw up" copious amounts of data is paramount to succeeding consistently. Refrain from going quickly and deeply into the details because, in this environment of information overload, our brains can only really absorb three concepts at once.

The cold statistics about facts and figures are that they land in our brain but drift away at varying speeds. But engaging, relatable stories that enter our mind will consistently take root and last longer.

And so it is the business differentiators – those who can take a personal story and relate it to the issues and needs of the person sitting on the other side of the table – who are succeeding faster and going further than their peers and competitors.

Now the good news is that everyone is a storyteller. We are hard-wired to tell and receive stories. The bad news is that many people are not entirely adequate at sharing a story that is compelling and relevant to a specific setting.

But do not be deterred. The art of linking clearly defined storytelling steps can be greatly improved with practice -- either alone, or in a team setting, to be more persuasive and effective in your presentations.

Harvest What Your Life Has Planted
List your most memorable life experiences that taught you something or changed your perspective on a matter. Practice extracting the true emotional connecting points that can be woven into a business story. Talk specifically about the actual emotion you felt - fear, anger, sadness, joy and use those emotions as anchors.

Walk A Mile In Their Shoes
Role play in a team setting as someone in a different occupation or avocation. Bring forth the mindset and temperament of what you believe this new position would require and foster in you. Speaking on a topic from a new point of view will help you see clearer what can make a story interesting, and reveal what is less than compelling!

Step Into The Spotlight

Display sincerity and transparency when telling an honest personal story. This will establish and strengthen a critical bond of trust that will be needed to make your point and get what you want.

You In A Word

List in a notebook (or on a whiteboard in a group session) adjectives you would use to describe your personal "brand." Jot down the descriptive words you believe others would offer to express what you project. Now list synonyms for the words on both lists and what emotions they produce.

Get It Ready For Broadway

Practice, practice, practice! Great storytellers make this powerful skill look easy, but it is honed through untold hours of rehearsal. Make sure the story that is presenting your message has been polished and is ready for the big stage.

Every day that you are gifted to walk this Earth, you are creating and attracting emotionally compelling stories. Make sure you work on cultivating them to be a vital part of leading and growing your business.

About Amy Posey

Amy Posey loves building leadership development experiences and sharing information about the brain to help people live more productive lives. She is a facilitator and CEO for Peak Teams based in San Jose, California.

Using the latest research in applied neuroscience, Amy creates and delivers innovative programs that help organizations grow their leadership. For the last six years at Peak Teams, she has designed leadership development experiences combining the adventure, neuroscience, and unique engaging techniques to accelerate business results for organizations of all sizes. Her client portfolio includes Adobe, Apple, BMC, Cisco, Dell-EMC, Hewlett-Packard, MasterCard, Microsoft, Time Warner, and VMware.

Prior to Peak Teams, Amy spent ten years at Deloitte, delivering internal leadership development programs, and learning, change, and communication solutions to global technology companies. Amy earned her B.A. in English, Education, and Writing from Purdue University and her M.B.A. in Managing Change and Marketing from DePaul University's campus in the Kingdom of Bahrain, where she lived and worked for two years.

She recently completed her Executive Masters with distinction from the Neuroleadership Institute. When not at work, Amy joins her husband, Bob, on spectacular paragliding hike-and-fly adventures to far-flung places across the globe.

Amy's Recommendations

Read One Book
Brain Rules by John Medina.
Learn more about how your brain works in a really accessible way.

Visit One Website
TED Talk: *"Stroke of Insight"* by Jill Bolte Taylor
Amercian author Jill Bolte Taylor shares what she learned about the different functions of our brain hemispheres after suffering a stroke.

Subscribe to One Podcast
Work Life with Adam Grant.
Go inside some of the world's most unusual workplaces to discover the keys to better work.

8

"Get comfortable with being uncomfortable."

Bill Eckstrom
Founder & President, EcSell Institute

Discomfort.

Competitive athletes know the value of it. Social activists embrace it. And butterflies may even understand the essence of it.

And that is if you want to get better; if you want to crush an entrenched negative behavior; or if you want to bring about a metamorphosis of profound change that maximizes your full potential, then you must get comfortable with being uncomfortable.

Because growth is a critical part of every competitive aspect of our world, the search for what fuels it is an ongoing journey. Growth is at the core of every business. All of the planning, all of the research, everything that everyone does, all revolves around the mantra that we want to grow.

However, the dichotomy is we are wired to pursue comfort and strive for order. People, by and large, would rather be comfortable and unhappy, then uncomfortable and happy.

But an exhaustive study conducted by the EcSell Institute in Lincoln, Nebraska, discovered that great companies, in addition to having good processes and strong trust-based relationships throughout its workforce, also created what can best be described as ...

... a healthy tension within their organization.

This wholesome discomfort exists individually and organizationally, and research of the coaches/managers of the performers and teams in the top 20% revealed these stark differences in comparison to their peers residing in the bottom 80%:

- They conduct 30% more coaching activities.
- They deliver 18% better quality coaching.
- They achieve 19% better in targeted goals (110% to goal vs 91%).
- They produce an average of $4.1 million in sales revenue.

Now, this is not a managerial license for boorish or mean-spirited behavior. Creating healthy discomfort is both a privilege and an obligation granted only after one has put in the time to get to know the other person.

The concept of "Growth Rings" is a clear illustration and application of the science of discomfort and growth. The Growth Rings represent our living environments that are either promoting or hindering growth.

The Growth Rings are represented by Chaos - Complexity - Order - Stagnation

Stagnation & Chaos
These two polar opposite rings both represent low performing, low growth environments. Stagnation is bogged down in minutiae that stifles creativity, independent thought and action (i.e., government work), and Chaos is whipped up by events or conditions and offers zero predictability or control over inputs or outcomes (i.e., mergers, natural disasters).

Order
Sits comfortably above Stagnation and takes pride in delivering predictable and favorable outcomes. But routine is the silent, deadly killer of future growth and prosperity.

Complexity

This ring is nothing more than changed Order. But when Order is disrupted, outcomes are no longer predictable, and unpredictability creates discomfort, which is where the stronger, better and transformed you, lies.

Now there are three primary ways to weave high-growth complexity into the fabric of your life:

It Can Forced Upon You

When an employer tells you, *'don't go away mad; just go away,'* you need to quickly get over the anger and fear of the dismissal and find the path that will have you one day saying, *'this was the best thing that could have ever happened to me!'*

Someone Can Help You Get There

A parent, mentor, teacher, or boss is a valued advisor for this role because left to our own devices we will consciously or subconsciously select the comfort of order.

You Can Trigger It Yourself

The chronicled history of our world and the record books of all sports are filled with individuals, groups, and teams who put their stake in the ground to do what most thought could never happen.

To be better and more comfortable with being uncomfortable, you might consider:
- Create a high-growth mindset by starting each day by reading something new.
- Spend time with people smarter than you.
- Ask more "why" questions than "how" questions.

Seeking discomfort is a challenge that defies our natural instincts, but we must learn to value it, embrace it and understand the essence of it because it is the only environment where sustained or exponential growth can occur.

About Bill Eckstrom

Bill Eckstrom has a passion - growth - especially how coaches and leaders impact the growth and performance of individuals and teams.

This passion inspired Bill to launch the EcSell Institute, a research-based organization that works with leaders internationally to help them better understand, measure, and elevate the impact coaching has on performance. EcSell's science and programming on the role of the coach has been changing behaviors, activities, and performance in diverse industries from athletic teams to businesses around the world.

Bill began his management career in 2000 at a medical equipment company and climbed the ranks to become US Director of Sales in just three years. In 2004, Bill accepted a job as Senior VP of Business Development for a publicly traded healthcare organization. By 2008, the organization's stock price had doubled and new sales revenue had grown 280%. Later that same year, he founded EcSell Institute.

As a result of his experiences and research, Bill's work as a keynote speaker is internationally renowned. He has presented to hundreds of groups and is a popular guest on podcasts and shows around the world. Bill was invited to the TEDx stage in 2017, and his talk entitled, "Why Comfort Will Ruin Your Life" is the fastest growing TEDx Talk in the history of the event.

Bill's home is in Nebraska, where he lives with his amazing wife, Kerstin. Together they have three children - Will Jr., Claire, and Maddie.

Bill's Recommendations

Read One Book
The Mindbody Prescription -- by Dr. John Sarno
This book takes an in depth look at the epidemic of debilitating pain. It identifies the root cause of pain disorders and how to treat them.

Visit One Website
PerformanceCoaching.ca
A dynamic speaker with a Ph.D in Sports Psychology, Peter Jensen brings innovative coaching techniques to boost personal performance in corporations worldwide.

Subscribe to One Podcast
Management Minutes
(Search on YouTube for the EcSell Institute Channel)
Quick hitting, informative segments about the impact coaching has on team performance and growth from VP of Sales, Will Kloefkorn, of the EcSell Institute.

9

"Measure your words for precise communication."

Jen Grogono
President & CEO
uStudio

In a comedy sketch on the long-running TV show, Saturday Night Live, a supervisor at a nuclear power plant leaves two new workers with one final reminder – *"And just remember; you can never put too much water in a nuclear reactor."* The pair of conscientious, but clearly overwhelmed workers then proceeded to comically debate whether the advice was a warning to never overfill the reactor, or simply a word of comfort to not worry about the amount of water they put into the nuclear furnace they were monitoring.

Oh, the perils and consequences of imprecise communication!

Not necessarily concise, but precise.

There are deeper layers to the seemingly obvious importance of effective communication. But do not confuse brevity with clarity. For instance, using vague words such as, 'roughly' or 'around' when scheduling a meeting time creates wide interpretation gaps that will undoubtedly result in wasted time and even missed opportunities.

When imprecise communication abounds and permeates an organization, it impacts the ability of its people to sell, support and service customers, and their ability to contribute to creating a culture of reliability.

Elevating the level of our communication lies in the trinity of our expression – our words; our tone and our body language – as noted in a study conducted by UCLA professor emeritus of Psychology, Albert Mehrabian.

Part of Mehrabian's research concluded that the non-verbal elements of communication are particularly important for conveying feelings and attitudes, especially when they do not match up with the stated words. When the words spoken do not align with the tone and posture of the speaker, the listener tends to believe the meaning expressed by the tonality and nonverbal behavior.

Professor Mehrabian quantified these "three V's" – Verbal, Vocal and Visual – in his findings known as the "7-38-55 Rule." Our processing of a person's message concerning their feelings breaks down that words account for 7%, tone of voice accounts for 38%, and body language accounts for 55% of our liking.

Technology has created seismic shifts in our ability to communicate more effectively and has catapulted us from the era of the printing press and delivering the written word in various formats, to the IoT (Internet of Things) and our ability to convey our message with powerful complementary forms of expression.

Now whether you choose to deliver your message with old-school print or amplify your announcement with technology, you will need to harness both with the "Three P's" – Planning, Preparation, and Practice – to make your communication clear and precise.

Plan
Simply the exercise of laying out the specific details of your message will identify the gaps in clarity that need to be reworked. Focus on the objective of your message and know your audience.

Prepare
Determine the main point of your message and state as precisely as possible. Put it up front and finish with it. Support the message with two or three strong facts that bolster your main point.

Practice
Whatever the platform – memo, video or presentation – put in the required time and effort to make the finished product flow smoothly and clearly. Enlist the help of others to gauge the clarity and impact of what you intend to deliver.

Be Multi-Modal

Leverage the free and easy use of web-conferencing tools to be able to assess the tone and body language of your audience's reception to your message. Print communication has its place for conveying an outline of steps or instructions to follow, but audio and visual aids are richer forms of communication to persuade and influence an audience.

Pick Up The Phone

Be mindful that tone and body language are missing from letters and emails, so reach out to the author to clarify their intent and meaning.

Now there may be some comedic debate on the ambiguity of tending to the water supply of a nuclear reactor, but there is no debate on the power of clear and precise communication in the business world!

About Jen Grogono

As Founder and Chief Executive Officer of uStudio Inc., Jen Grogono leads company vision and strategy for a new generation of enterprise communications software that uses podcasting, live and on-demand video to radically improve productivity, accelerate sales, and transform customer relationships.

In 2006, Ms. Grogono founded one of the first multi-channel media networks, On Networks (ON), where she served as President and Chief Content Officer. Under her leadership, ON pioneered new forms of digital programming, any-screen distribution, media marketing and monetization, partnering with blue-chip brands, agencies and a virtual team of original content creators.

Prior to On Networks, Ms. Grogono spent more than 15 years creating and implementing strategic marketing programs across a range of technology, consumer and public service organizations.

Ms. Grogono served as vice president of corporate marketing for Motive Inc. (now Alcatel), where she handled pre-and post-IPO marketing, public relations and investor communications. She has also held GM and executive positions at Porter Novelli, an Omnicom-owned worldwide firm; Kurion, a digital content and application syndication company (acquired by iSyndicate, now Yellowbrix); and Lois Paul & Partners.

A cum laude graduate of Boston College, Jen Grogono is a frequent speaker at events such as SXSW and NAB on the intersection of media and technology. Her early work in digital media has been recognized through industry awards and noted in business publications like the New York Times, Fortune, and The Wall Street Journal. She contributed to Peachpit Press's new media book, *Web Video: Making it Great, Getting it Noticed*

Jen's Recommendations

Read One Book
The Carrot Seed by Ruth Krauss
A beautifully simple story that teaches patience and the technique of planting a seed to help it grow. First published in 1945, this timeless classic has never been out of print.

Visit One Website
ustudio.com
A valued corporate partner that will help improve productivity, accelerate sales and transform customer relationships.

Subscribe To One Podcast
npr.org/podcasts/510298/ted-radio-hour
The TED Radio Hour is a journey through fascinating ideas, astonishing inventions, fresh approaches to old problems and new ways to think or create.

10

"If you can draw it, they will do it."

Tim Riesterer
Chief Strategy Officer
Corporate Visions

Aristotle said, *'the soul never thinks without a picture,'* and we could add to the words of the great Greek philosopher and scientist, 'the mind doesn't make a decision without one either.'

If you are a team leader or a sales executive, you will be significantly more effective if presentations are rooted in visual over verbal persuasion.

Studies show that pictures have proven to be worth more than the old adage of a thousand words.

The **Picture Superiority Effect** refers to the phenomenon in which pictures and images are remembered more than words. This effect has been vividly demonstrated in numerous experiments, including one that presented information orally to people, in which the participants only remembered about 10% three days later. However, when an image – photo or drawing – is incorporated into a presentation, the recall rate three days later skyrockets to about 65%.

Underscoring the importance of visual messaging over verbal persuasion is the science of how we make our decisions.

Showing is better than telling.

We know the part of the brain that fires and causes people to make a change does not contain the capacity for language. The capacity for language is in the rational or logical part of the brain that people use to justify and validate a decision. But the actual decision to change occurs in the part of the brain that does not have the ability to process language.

So the 'weapon of choice' for all presentations should be pen and paper over PowerPoint!

With this better understanding of the roles neuroscience, social psychology and behavioral economics play in the decision-making process that shapes how people reach their conclusions, it is incumbent upon team leaders and sales executives to embrace these hidden forces and meticulously create, as well as persuasively deliver, their message of change.

This is accomplished by converting the specific corporate message from an abstract and complicated problem into a simple and concrete task.

Now the goal for all 'change scenarios' is to **tell a story that will persuade and influence someone to do something different tomorrow then they are doing today.** We are asking the customer, prospect or department team to give up their current status quo approach, for a new alternative approach.

And this story must be believable, achievable and draw-able!

So with a simple concrete drawn visual, show your audience the broken current state, and then contrast that with a new and better state which fixes the problem.

We know that the biggest lever that the brain uses to make decisions is contrast. It makes an emotional and intuitive decision to change based on the contrast between what it is doing today and what it is being asked to do tomorrow. And it is in this contrast where you need to show your audience the value of making the change you are presenting.

There are three steps to ready yourself for this personal change in presentation style away from digital (PowerPoint) to analog storytelling.

1) Take an existing story and redraw it on a whiteboard, flipchart or napkin. Practice with something familiar or a story you have told many times. Convert these ideas into a cohesive "flow" that can be told in a drawing.

2) Practice with your peers. Try running your next team meeting or internal executive meeting by using ONLY the whiteboard. Leverage this safe audience to garner feedback on style, clarity and effectiveness --- before you

test the waters with a real customer.

3) Ditch the Laptop. When you go into the next important presentation, trade in your set of PowerPoint slides for a colorful assortment of erasable markers to make your case.

We have drawn, no pun intended, a clear and scientifically based roadmap that will assist team leaders and sales executives in creating and delivering more effective presentations.

If you can draw the change you are proposing, your audience will do it!

About Tim Reisterer

Tim, a sought-after consultant on the important dynamics of improving corporate messaging, wastes no time in sharing his ONE THING that will enhance a person's sales and leadership skills.

Tim Riesterer has dedicated his career to improving the conversations companies have with prospects and customers.

He is a researcher and co-author of three books on the subject – *Customer Message Management; Conversations That Win The Complex Sale;* and *The Three Value Conversations.*

Tim has also consulted and trained the top companies in the world on how to improve their messaging development and delivery. As Chief Strategy Officer for Corporate Visions, he sets the direction and develops products for this leading marketing and sales messaging, tools and training company.

Tim's Recommendations

Read One Book
The Three Value Conversations by Erik Petersen and Tim Riesterer. How to Create, Elevate, and Capture customer value at every stage of the long-lead sale.

Visit One Website
CorporateVisions.com
A site that will help you create winning sales conversations.

Subscribe to One Podcast
corporate vision.com/content-library/
An expansive collection of webinars that will help align you closer with customers.

11

"Make it safe for people to explore their own thinking."

Alan Fine
Founder and President
InsideOut Development

The subjective opinion of most people in leadership positions is that they foster a healthy working environment where employees feel free to express themselves on matters of their work.

No doubt, you would be hard-pressed to find a company that boasts of their "closed-door policy" on the topic of input from staffers. But actions speak louder than words, and every leader needs to have an accurate assessment of the impact they have on the corporate culture when it comes to maximizing the abilities of their staff.

Learning stops when defenses go up.

When workers do not feel safe, they will invariably put up their defenses. Once this happens; all learning stops. It is a natural human instinct that is best to avoid rather than trying to undo.

SayDoCo

The most crucial driver of performance is personal accountability. Succinctly stated, **say what you'll do; and do what you say.**

There is a critical third part to this axiom, and that is everyone - CEO, manager, staffer - needs to **feel comfortable to communicate** when they find they can't do what they say they will do. Easily stated as "SayDoCo."

Unless people feel safe to speak freely, they won't share bad news. Rather, they will cover up the problem and will rationalize their actions by shifting the blame to the "kill the messenger" culture they believe exists.

Make it safe for people to explore their own thinking.

But leaders practicing this trinity of "SayDoCo" and who genuinely invite others to embrace it, will begin to pull out the weeds of skepticism and scapegoating. Growing in their place will be seeds of trust and personal accountability to grow a more nurturing culture.

This will happen when conversations between colleagues, and between supervisors and subordinates, have three critical elements: **Candor -- Caring -- Constructive.**

All discussions must be an open and honest expression of thoughts with a sincere desire to be respectful of opposing viewpoints while serving a useful purpose of coming to a specific best solution.

A simple but powerfully effective way to maximize every conversation is to use a method employed by pilots, surgeons and others in high-stress occupations -- work from a checklist.

The **G.R.O.W. Model**™ serves as a conversation checklist that will ensure each party is entering into a safe exchange of ideas. It's an acronym that represents the four components of any decision-making process.

> **G:** Clearly state the **GOAL** you seek to achieve.
> **R:** Understand the **REALITIES** that exist in the context of the decision process.
> **O:** Consider the **OPTIONS** available to the decision-maker.
> **W:** Set a **WAY FORWARD** – the specific action plan for each step to achieve success.

This road-tested questioning model will guide practitioners through the critical elements of the decision-making process and create action that will deliver results.

G.R.O.W. is a process model, so people can have different goals when they begin a discussion and will be reassured they are entering a zone of mutual respect for differing viewpoints through each step.

Write the words, **CANDOR, CARING** and **CONSTRUCTIVE** at the top of an index card, and list below the words, **GOAL, REALITY, OPTIONS,** and **WAY FORWARD** to serve as a close-at-hand checklist when having a conversation with a coworker or client.

Offer, and hopefully receive empathetic listening, will provide a level of safety and demonstrate a willingness to describe different perspectives on the matter at hand.

Continued practice of this method will ensure a measure of comfort knowing that you are on a proven track that will deliver a **WAY FORWARD** to an equitable solution.

Implement the four phases of **G.R.O.W.** to create the focus required for better, faster decision-making and outstanding performance. By establishing an environment that allows people to feel safe to explore their own thinking, the work setting becomes an incubator for maximizing employee potential and performance.

About Alan Fine

Alan is considered the pioneer of the modern-day coaching movement and is the co-creator of the widely recognized GROW® Model. Alan is a New York Times Bestselling Author, international performance expert, sought-after keynote speaker, and well-respected business executive and professional athlete coach. He has dedicated the past 35 years to helping people from all walks of life to elevate their performance and unlock potential. From the golf course to the boardroom, Alan has worked with many of the world's most respected athletes and organizations.

Inspired by a powerful personal performance breakthrough on the tennis court, Alan has refined and honed his coaching model into a profoundly simple and highly effective approach for improving individual and team performance—known as the InsideOut Approach. Alan's work with the InsideOut Approach has touched the lives of athletes such as Davis Cup tennis star Buster Mottram, world record-breaking triathlete James Lawrence, and PGA golfers Phillip Price, David Feherty, Colin Montgomerie, and Stephen Ames; and has significantly impacted the organizational culture and business results of companies like IBM, Goodyear, Gap, and Coca-Cola.

Alan's thought leadership on the nature of performance and the art of coaching for performance improvement, includes his New

York Times Bestselling book—*You Already Know How to be Great*, as well as numerous other research articles and publications, and the proprietary content of InsideOut Development solutions portfolio.

Alan's Recommendations

Read One Book
Untethered Soul - Michael Singer
In this NY Times bestseller, author and spiritual teacher, Michael Singer explores the question of who we are.

Visit One Website
Seth Godin.com
The destination to tap into information on Seth Godin's 18 bestselling books; 8 online courses; and more than 7,00 blog posts.

Subscribe to One Podcast
Friday Night Comedy From BBC Radio 4
Tune in and enjoy the topical satire and offbeat comedy on BBC Radio 4.

12

"Develop quality personal relationships to enhance your business success."

Mala Grewal
Founder & CEO
Talent Catalyst

Delivering an exceptional performing product or service at a fair competitive price surrounded by dedicated customer service are undoubtedly critical ingredients that feed the growth of businesses, both big and small. However, it is the quality of our personal relationships with clients and prospects that provides the fertile soil in which all individual and corporate success grows.

Make no mistake, the good fortune of businesses begin and end with developing and maintaining quality relationships.

Nowadays we are constantly being lured into the time-sapping traps of technology – growing your social media platform – and sent down the path of the latest seminar teachings that will build your brand and strengthen your skills.

Good intentions will all fall short of their potential without real and meaningful business relationships.

It is the social dynamic of relationships that are both the fuel and lubricant that powers all phases of business and keeps it running smoothly.

Before you can demonstrate your business prowess, you must be able to effectively communicate with a potential employer that you are the right person for the job. **A Harvard University study found that 85% of professional success comes from people skills,** and only 15% of why a person gets a job, retains or advances in that job is related to their technical skills or job knowledge.

And once you get your foot in the door, it will be your ability to foster quality relationships with superiors that will be the image of difference in your career. A study conducted in conjunction with a business professor at the University of Virginia showed that "as much as 90% of the information that the most senior executives of a company receive and take action on comes through their informal networks, and not from formal reports and databases."

Now securing the job and then the respect of your employer will earn you the privilege of maintaining the company's business with existing customers while capturing new market share from the competition.

And the decisions of buyers have provided ample evidence that it is not always the best product or service, or the best price, that wins the day. It will be your ability to create a relationship that is bonded by a mixture of trust, respect, and compatibility.

Once you commit to the delicate balancing act of putting in the required time to strengthening existing business relationships and investing in creating new ones, it will be a watershed moment in your career.

Set Connection Goals
Because what gets measured gets done, set a weekly goal to speak with at least two key contacts at existing accounts and set the table to have an introductory conversation with at least two prospective clients. Use Linkedin as a tool to build meaningful relationships.

Be An Honest Expert
Your client or prospect will assume you are well-versed in your product and their business. But admit when you don't have an answer to a question an honor your promise to get back with a response.

Give More Than You Get
Don't only call when YOU need something. Relationships grow deep and strong when your mission is to learn the customer's wants, needs, and dreams, and then find an opportunity to satisfy them.

Be Transparent and Proactive

Focus on stimulating conversations around goals and expectations. Use your journal notes and knowledge gleaned from the blossoming relationship to articles, links, and related information to the customer's interests. This is an image-of-difference strategy that will repay your effort many times over.

Be At Your Best When The Worst Happens

When mistakes happen, offer a sincere straight-forward apology without adding any negative comments leveled about your employer. And be ready with a detailed plan to remedy the problem. In the aftermath of any fury raised, it will be your professional demeanor and plan to get back on track that will remain.

So if you want to grow your business, make sure the soil you work in is rich in quality relationships!

About Mala Grewal

Mala is a successful Executive Facilitator, Coach, and Change Management Consultant. Her dedication to solving business challenges combined with her innate ability to intuit development possibility within individuals allows her to deliver sustainable transformation with clients.

Mala began her career consulting officer teams on change initiatives with the United States Navy, as well as coaching executives on career transition and development. She continued her change work at the world's leading general aviation firm, Universal Weather and Aviation. Mala went on to become a Regional Vice President Partners in Leadership, coaching senior leadership teams on how to build and manage cultures of accountability to deliver on key business results. Most recently she has facilitated digital immersion and leadership in a digital age programs for Visa and Nestle global teams.

Mala currently runs Talent Catalyst, a career performance consultancy committed to connecting Millennials to their highest performance in a measurable way. Mala has a charismatic and powerful presence in front of crowds. Her background in theater and vocal performance, along with enthusiasm, sense of humor, and curiosity for life, make her a dynamic hit with her audience.

Mala's Recommendations

Read One Book
Rework by Jason Fried
This book has something new to say about building, running, and growing (or not growing) a business.

Visit One Website
TalentCatalyst.com
Dynamic, high-energy experiences focused on participatory teaching methodologies.

Subscribe to One Podcast
On Being by Krista Tippet
Pursuing deep thinking, social change, moral imagination and joy, to renew inner life, out life and life together.

13

"Lead with vulnerability."

Chris Kelly
Co-Founder & Vice Chairman
Convene

In his novel, *Norwegian Wood,* Haruki Murakami offers a profoundly simple answer to the eternally complex question of, *"What happens when people open their hearts?"*

The acclaimed Japanese author succinctly states, *"They get better."*

In many ways, we have been programmed to believe that expressing our vulnerability is a clear sign of weakness and confessing to an imperfection. And doing so on the job would be tantamount to career suicide.

But the high tide of such antiquated thinking has been steadily retreating back to whence it came and is not likely to return. People are enjoying the rewards of deep and meaningful connections in their personal and professional relationships that are formed when they demonstrate the courage to be vulnerable.

Work to make strong connections with customers, to build trust and become more than just a vendor selling something.

Brene Brown, an expert on the subject of social connections and who embraces the label of 'respected researcher and skilled storyteller,' concludes after conducting thousands of interviews that vulnerability is at the heart of all social connections. People having the courage to put down their shields of pretense and false bravado to reveal their authentic self.

As leaders and individual contributors we have been conditioned to keep a professional distance and maintain an appearance of confidence and competence. Many times we fear sharing any vulnerability could be weaponized and used against us. But the research shows this is typically not the case.

Psychologist and author, Adam Grant's research shows that you can reverse the 'nice guys finish last' adage, provided the courageous and generous person expressing their vulnerability manages their empathy; sets limits on their availability and works to overcome their timidity.

When leaders are willing to step towards understanding vulnerability they are moving in a transformative direction. Trust and transparency are the healthy by-products of vulnerability and they are the vital nutrients that will create a fertile environment for individual and corporate growth.

When it comes to innovation and organizational growth, it is all about being vulnerable. Only the most courageous leaders are measured with this "vulnerability yardstick."

Seemingly vulnerable phrases like, 'I don't know,' 'I was wrong,' and 'I'm sorry' are really statements of strength.

Continuing on this parallel dichotomy of strength coming from the perception of vulnerability, we learn the perhaps initially painful but ultimately joyous life lesson, that to obtain what we want the most, we need to be vulnerable to what we fear the most.

In an effort to illuminate the dark untraveled path of voluntary vulnerability, you might consider trying these exercises:

Destigmatize Vulnerability
Take the lead and start with yourself. Be open, transparent and share your vulnerabilities with the team to spark the conversation.

Start Each Meeting With a Moment of Transparency
Open up team meetings with each person sharing one item where they were successful, and one item where they got stuck and felt vulnerable.

Exercise The Vulnerability Muscle
There are many great skills that can be practiced (and exercised) in a team setting. Google search with keywords -"dare to lead workbook" and you will find many of Brene' Brown's ideas that can easily be incorporated into your next group meeting.

Just Sit and Listen
When leaders keep their ego in check and let the energy of others flow in meetings, is when productivity rises. Be conscious to not drive every conversation. Let the team share their visions and their ideas on how to solve current obstacles. Ask more questions versus providing answers.

Take The Challenge
Be willing to accept tough questions and offer back answers that are genuinely respectful and authentic, based on the knowledge at hand. Do not view this as a challenge to your authority or values.

Embracing these prescriptive tactics will answer quite clearly the question of, what happens when people open their hearts – they get better!

About Chris Kelly

Chris Kelly is the Co-Founder and Vice Chairman, of Convene. The company designs and services a network of premium places to work, meet, and host inspiring events. Convene has raised $260M in equity funding to date, and has been named one of America's 100 Most Promising Companies by Forbes and a Best Workplace by both Inc. and Fortune Magazine.

Chris has been individually recognized as CoreNet Global's 2018 Young Leader of the Year, CoreNet NYC's 2017 Service Provider of the Year, on Real Estate Forum's 50 Under 40 List, as an EY Entrepreneur of the Year Semi-Finalist, and the only person to be named to Inc. Magazine's 30 Under 30 list twice.

Chris's Recommendations

Read One Book
*The 46 Rules of Genius: An Innovator's Guide To Creativity
(Voices That Matter)* by Marty Neumeier
A genius is anyone that turns insight into innovation, and in the process changes our view of the world.

Visit One Website
Seth Godin's Blog Site -- https://seths.blog/
The destination to tap into more than 7,00 blog posts.

Subscribe to One Podcast
The Tim Ferriss Show-- https://tim.blog/podcast/
Tim's show is often rated the #1 business podcast on all of Apple Podcasts, and it has been ranked #1 out of 500,000 podcasts on many occasions.

14

"To drive performance, detach from the goal and focus on the process."

Scott Edinger
CEO, Edinger Consulting

When the Zen-like thinking that, 'success is a journey and not a destination' runs head-on into the pragmatic resolve to keep a laser focus on a specific goal to achieve it, there is bound to be some pause to which is the correct path.

There is strength in numbers to support the wisdom of setting and closely tracking specific, actionable goals. But give serious consideration to a counterintuitive approach that orients your work around a goal, but dials back the call to obsess over it on a daily basis.

When you put the Zen-stones away and begin to prioritize the process to achieve your objective, over continually staring down the road to the end goal, you will realize that it is the daily execution of your action plan that will determine the degree of speed, comfort, and success of your journey.

Let's take it one play at a time.

Sports has long been a dominant part of our culture, and whether as a participant or a spectator, you undoubtedly have heard coaches and players talk about breaking games and seasons down into the tiniest of segments.

The goal of winning a game can only be reached when the process of flawlessly executing each offensive and defensive play is achieved. A team can only win a championship by winning the requisite number of games in the series and doing it one game at a time. And stringing postseason victories together is accomplished by winning a sufficient number of in-game battles.

In a corporate world, the scoreboard that often dominates our thoughts is a forecast or sales quota. And as in sports, 'the score will take care of itself' if we shift our attention to designing a process for success and put into practice what you have carefully planned. This approach serves to do more than simply set you on a path to reach a long-term goal. In the short run, this new mindset will choke off bad habits and strengthen new and improved ones with steady daily doses of positive reinforcement.

It is when you change things at the process stage and focus on designing the best road to travel to the desired results, and methodically track your path to progress, that you will consistently and successfully arrive at the goal stage.

The devil is in the details.

For those who do not recognize the importance of setting and following a detailed plan, they will undoubtedly have a devil of a time achieving their goal. Writing down your goal is universally accepted as an important first step to achieving it. But if you want to dramatically improve your chances of staying motivated and on track to reach your goal, then you need to **live in the details of the blueprint** you meticulously take the time to create.

It is steady completion of each successive day's planned work that will transport you to your destination. This is the work of an active goal setter. Often they leave behind their passive goal-setting colleagues or competitors who gaze excitedly at the finish line off in the distance. These folks will race out of the starting blocks, but quickly lose their enthusiasm and inevitably their way.

Here's how to detach from your goals and focus on the process.

Manage your time.

You must harness the hours in every day to work for you, or your goals will be nothing more than strong desires. Consider taking inventory of your daily tasks and list them in one of four quadrants:

Urgent, but Not Important
(upper left)

Urgent and Important
(upper right)

Not Urgent and Not Important
(bottom left)

Not Urgent, but Important
(bottom right)

Being a great "time manager" means you must learn to be effective and efficient. You must win the challenge to spend your time on the things that are important (tasks on the right side of the quadrant), and not just the ones that are urgent and keep demanding your attention.

Practice the V2MOM model.

This is a powerful management process for effective goal setting and organizational alignment created by Salesforce co-founder and CEO, Marc Benioff. V2MOM is an acronym for **Visions, Values, Methods, Obstacles, and Measures.** With the last component of the model – Measures – you are asked to clearly define what you are going to focus on to achieve your goal and establish an indicator of your progress. The V2MOM model urges you to set a goal that is challenging, yet achievable and to be certain your standard for measuring is consistent with your company's measures.

Going forward there will be ample time to enjoy the view when you successfully get to your destination. But the surest way to guarantee an on-time arrival is to keep your eyes on the road that is in front of you.

About Scott Edinger

Companies like AT&T, Lenovo, McDonalds, and *The Los Angeles Times,* hire Scott Edinger to help them lead revenue growth. Scott works with senior leaders to develop strategies and execute approaches that achieve increased top and bottom line results. As a consultant, author, advisor, and speaker, he creates positive change for clients, and is recognized as an expert on leadership for revenue growth.

Scott's latest book, *The Hidden Leader: Discover And Develop Greatness Within Your Company* (AMACOM, 2015) is a Washington Post Bestseller, and was selected as one of the best business books of 2015. He is also co-author of, *The Inspiring Leader* (McGraw-Hill 2009), and the Harvard Business Review article, *Making Yourself Indispensable,* called by HBR a "classic in the making." Scott is also a regular contributor to Forbes and the Harvard Business Review, in addition to being an affiliate faculty member for the University of North Carolina, Keenan-Flagler School of Business.

Scott received a B.S. in rhetoric and communication studies from Florida State University. Scott gives back to the FSU community by serving on alumni committees including the Board of the College of Communication and Information, and Seminole Torchbearers.

Although he cannot read music and is not a Mormon, he has performed with the Mormon Tabernacle Choir. Scott and his family live in Tampa, Florida.

Scott's Recommendations

Read One Book
Meditations by Marcus Aurelius
A series of personal writings by Marcus Aurelius, Roman
Emperor 161-180 BC, setting forth his ideas on Stoic philosophy.

Visit One Website
EdingerConsulting.com
The Edinger Consulting team provides leadership strategies for
revenue growth.

Subscribe to One Podcast
2Bobs -- With David C. Baker and Blair Enns
Conversations on the art of creative entrepreneurship.

15

"You have to take risks."

Donal Daly
Chief Rocket Launcher
6 Rockets

It has been said that the only true risk in life is not taking any chances. Playing it safe, or a strategy of inertia and procrastination in our fast-changing world does not lead to greatness. It more reliably has proven to deliver mediocrity or underperformance.

To be clear, we are not referring to a reckless, "ready, fire, aim" strategy. But rather a calculated leap to a destination clearly seen but perhaps not always fully understood. This leap includes:

- Carefully analyzing your skill set to start any daunting task.
- Assessing the 'in the air' learning curve that will undoubtedly take place once you make the jump.
- Measuring the depth of your passion, patience, and persistence to fuel the requisite fighting spirit needed to make dreams happen.

Now undoubtedly there is an event or two in every person's life where we regret taking a chance that did not turn out as hoped. We are in fact richer for those experiences. More often, we regret the moments that we did not take that leap even when we were not entirely sure what was on the other side.

Take a risk or lose the chance.

Many individuals and companies in the technology sector might be characterized as, 'riskaholics.' They thrive on the next risk, obstacles and challenges to be overcome.

But that is the thing about risk; it travels this road of life with a companion named, ambition. While incremental changes can happen in a safe way, BIG ambition demands a willingness to take a risk. If you want something to be transformational, to change your life, your career, your business, then you need to think BIG -- face down risk -- and figure out how to deal with it.

With the rapid change that is taking place all around us, organizations (and teams) must embrace the revelation where status quo is not an option. Strive for transformational change at every turn. The need to take risks is really the driver of the entrepreneurial attitude and initiative demanded by the current maelstrom of technological advances.

It is easier, and perhaps in the short-run safer, to settle for mediocrity. But if you want to get ahead of the pack, if you want to be an anomaly, then you have to act like one. Achieving goals, both professional and personal, demands that you take positive calculated risk.

And while with any risk there is always something at stake to lose or dramatically alter; there are also huge benefits to stepping out and taking a calculated chance.

Top ten benefits of taking a risk.

1. Forces you to learn new skills.
2. Helps you to overcome the fear of failure.
3. Empowers you to break through self-imposed limits.
4. Makes you more creative.
5. Will clarify what you really want.
6. Helps you break free from the mindset of being 'average.'
7. Will uncover unforeseen opportunities.
8. Stimulates and strengthens your self-confidence.
9. Necessitates that you learn to trust more.
10. Is the only path to achieve your dreams.

As you review the list, notice that risk actually produces positive "updates" that shape your mindset. This can transform you into a more dynamic and successful leader or executive.

But there is another side to the coin -- not taking a risk (or your moon shot). Ironically, with this choice you run the bigger risk of being left behind. Without intervention - situations rarely improve. Time in fact does not heal everything. In many cases, situations that are neglected or ignored will decay or build to become an even bigger problem.

Too often many people focus on what might go wrong and by default choose the path of least resistance as the best option, and hope for the best. Top leaders run hard to get away from mediocrity, to get ahead and to fulfill their dreams and ambitions. They consider the impossible, contemplate the risk, and then take that leap to break from the pack.

So ready, aim, and fire...Take your best shot!

About Donal Daly

In 1986 Donal Daly started his quest to improve human performance with his first Artificial Intelligence software company. In 2005, he founded Altify, his fifth global company, to improve sales performance through software. He is regarded as the catalyst for global advancement in sales transformation.

Donal is a sought-after speaker and business strategist. An engineer from University College Cork in Ireland, he has split his time over the last 30 years between Europe and the United States, always curious and always learning. His most recent concerns and areas of focus are the decline in critical thinking and the danger of the inherent biases in the AI algorithms powering some of the world's largest companies.

Donal is the author of multiple Amazon best sellers including, *Digital Sales Transformation in a Customer First World; Tomorrow Today: How AI Impacts How We Work, Live and Think; and Account Planning in Salesforce.* His ideas, books, and speeches have inspired people around the world to perform better.

Donal's Recommendations

Read One Book
Digital Sales Transformation In A Customer First World
by Donal Daly
This book offers a digital sales transformation blueprint to guide sales organizations to help better respond to business disruptions.

Visit One Website
DonalDaly.com
"Think for a Living" is Donal's collection of blog posts, articles, books and videos.

Subscribe to One Podcast
The Best of AI
https://player.fm/podcasts/Ai
Explore the world of Artificial Intelligence from industry leading experts.

16

"Failure is the tuition for success."

Colin Nanka
Senior Director, Sales Enablement
Salesforce

Success is rarely a straight line to the top right quadrant of your life graph.

There are inevitable blips up and down. Every team leader or sales executive should pack an ample supply of resilience to have any chance at long-term success.

History, and likely our own personal experience, shows us that quite often professional breakthroughs come in the down dips.

Perhaps the patron saint of resilience and the ultimate learner from failure was Thomas Edison. This great inventor is known to have made thousands of prototypes of the light bulb before he got it right. And with more than 1,000 patents awarded to him, it is awe-inspiring to consider all of the failures that paid the tuition for his portfolio of successful protected inventions.

Now in moments of failure, it will take more than just telling yourself (or someone else) to *'toughen up and work harder.'*

No, the disclaimer here is that bounce backs occur in setback moments.

If failure is the tuition you pay for success, are you making enough deposits?

Pride and courage are needed to evaluate our approach and attitude that perhaps got us into a slump. In addition, spirit and tenacity will be required to implement the necessary changes to get back up and push forward. Because more than technical skills or business connections, it is the ability to endure the inevitable times of adversity, that will produce the adjusted high-level effort required. This will allow your talents and relationships to flourish and be a catalyst for success.

No doubt it is easy to 'feed the bank' when things are rolling along nicely. But we need objective strategies to rely on that will ignite and strengthen our resiliency when we derail or go into a downward spiral.

Major In The Major

When failure arrives, **do not get bogged down** in the minor issues of the problem at hand.
Step back from the trouble and focus your energy and intellect on identifying the main parts of the problem that you *can* control.

This Too Shall Pass

Strengthen your resolve by **stepping away** from the business crisis and remind yourself this is not a fatal condition or a criminal matter.

Refuse to be buried under fear and indecision. Calm your thoughts and practice telling yourself that failure is a learning moment and a chance to grow stronger. The goal here is to steadily push through it.

Put On A Happy Face

Step outside of yourself and **choose an optimistic approach** to rectify the problem. Choosing to feed the fire of failure with abrasive and derogatory language towards yourself, peers or subordinates is ultimately a losing proposition.

Raison D'Etre

Focus on YOUR reason for being. Identify *'why you do what you do'* and **anchor yourself** to it when failure crashes down. Resilience is easier to muster when you are passionate about the problem that needs fixing. Conversely, it is very difficult to bring a *'refuse to lose'* spirit to a project where commitment is lacking.

It is through the repetition of resilience-building strategies like these four igniters that the resolve muscles will strengthen to help successfully pivot away from failure.

Objectively we are paying the right price by being uncomfortable in a task or moment at hand. See it for what is – an opportunity for growth.

In these crucial moments of life and business, we come to understand that hard work is a given for any chance at success, and that the road to victory almost always detours through failure. From this starting point, we must incorporate the strategies for resilience that are sustaining and allow us to pay the price for success!

About Colin Nanka

Colin is the Senior Director, Sales Enablement for North American Sales and Leadership Development at the world's leading Customer Relationship Management Company, Salesforce.com.

He is a proven sales leader with over twenty years of experience including time at Salesforce and Xerox Corporation. Colin completed his business degree in Canada at the University of Alberta.

In his spare time, he competes in multi-day, self-sustained, adventure races in the world's most treacherous terrains, including the Sahara Desert, Gobi Desert, Iceland, Grand Canyon, Atacama Desert, Antarctica and, most recently, in Patagonia.

He has a passion for writing, collaborating, learning and empowering his community to go further.

Explore and subscribe to Colin's adventures and inspirational blog by visiting ColinNanka.com.

Colin's Recommendations

Read One Book

How Champions Think by Dr. Bob Rotella
An acclaimed sports psychologist, Bob Rotella, offers
groundbreaking advice applicable to elite performers and
everyday business people on how to flourish under pressure and
overcome challenges.

Visit One Website

ColinNanka.com
A website that will provide inspiration and insight to defeat
average every day.

Subscribe To One Podcast

The New York Times
A daily news podcast and radio show by the respected American
newspaper.

17

"You owe it to yourself, to know yourself."

Brenda Jo March
Founder & CEO
March Forward Consulting

Many personal development experts stress the importance of being authentic.

Quite often, we use this word as an adjective to confirm that an item is real or true, but we don't generally think of this quality in relation to ourselves. In order to be authentic, you must **fully develop your self-awareness**.

Self-awareness is not taught in most academic programs because many believe it happens organically throughout your lifetime. If this holds true, individuals can activate self-discovery to increase their personal success.

In sales, you were likely told that people buy from people they know, like, and trust. Another person can only get to "know" you if you "know" yourself. People "like" people they have something in common with. So active listening and sharing your common core values, passions, and interests are important. Establishing "trust" requires that you create consistency, be self-aware and help others recognize what they can expect from you.

If people like you, they'll listen to you. But if they trust you, they'll do business with you.

Use these three 'C' words to strengthen your self-awareness:

Clarity
Self-awareness requires you to clearly recognize your personal values, intentions and goals. Neuroscience has proven that documenting your thoughts, core values, intentions, and goals encodes them in your brain. Encoding sends these ideas to the brain's hippocampus to be analyzed and stored. When documented, the brain processes twice -- once as a thought and then again when it's written down.

As we consider the words to express thoughts, additional cognitive processes are occurring in the brain making it more memorable. As individuals become more clear about who they are, it's easier to articulate thoughts to colleagues and customers. Finding clarity around what matters to you will result in a less reactive and more consistent business presence. The true benefit is that you will stand out from the crowd as someone who is self-assured with clarity.

Commitment

As you begin to develop a sense of self-awareness, schedule time on a regular basis to self-reflect and write down what matters. Consider situations that have happened during the week and whether or not you were true to your core values, intentions, and goals. If you were true (to you), reward yourself and consider ways to enhance that behavior. If you were reactive in a situation and didn't behave in the way you would have liked, consider how to potentially correct the situation or ways to avoid this behavior in the future.

Consider developing an accountability partner relationship (with a peer) to hold each other accountable for both of your personal development journeys. This is a true commitment.

Consistency

Neuropsychological research proves humans desire certainty. Certainty activates the brain's positive "reward" response versus the "threat" response causing fear and distrust.

Being able to anticipate how you will behave in a situation is powerful in challenging circumstances. When a colleague can anticipate how you are likely to respond based on consistent behavior, it allows them to easily collaborate in reaching complex goals. Becoming self-aware drives consistency in developing a trusted relationship.

Give these exercises the time and energy that they deserve.

Becoming self-aware is an empowering investment in future success, both professionally and personally. In the business world, understand that customers will know if you are disingenuous with overall effort, product and service claims. Ask the question, *"why would a customer buy from me if I wouldn't buy from myself?"*

Being true to yourself in all aspects of life starts with knowing yourself first!

About Brenda Jo March

Brenda March is a Certified Performance Coach, founder of March Forward Consulting, and author of, *The Project of You: Beyond High School*, which presents guidelines to emerging adults for creating a plan for their future by utilizing five key success skills to address challenges along the way.

As a coach, author, mentor, speaker, connector, and consultant, Brenda draws upon her 30 plus years of counseling, business communication and technology consulting experience to passionately provide individual and group coaching.

Brenda's additional publishing credits include, *The Woman's Guide for Self-Esteem: How to Build Confidence* and *Young Empowered Speakers Guide to Develop and Use Your Unique Voice*. Brenda oversees the Young Empowered Speakers Program to help young adults find and use their voice through public speaking and volunteers annually at the Pennsylvania Free Enterprise Week (PFEW) conference. To learn more, visit *www.marchforwardconsulting.com*

Brenda Jo's Recommendations

Read One Book
Be Yourself, Everyone Else is Already Taken: Transform Your Life with the Power of Authenticity by Mike Robbins
A great read to assist you to access your true self and how to use that to develop the relationships you crave at work, at home, and with yourself.

Visit One Website
LiveYourLegend.net
Chelsea Dinsmore continues Scott's legacy and this site provides discovery packs, courses, and inspiration to assist you in your self-awareness journey.

Subscribe To One Podcast
Simon Sinek's "Start with Why"
Simon guides you to greater self-awareness and also helps you delve into why you do -- what you do.

18

"Use the phrase, 'tell me more' every chance you can."

Ashley Welch
Co-Founder
Somersault Innovation

The Greek philosopher, Epictetus, is credited with saying, *'God gave us two ears and one mouth, so we should listen twice as much as we speak.'*

Admittedly, the Stoic sage had the luxury of likely never having to hit a sales quota. But for those leaders and sales executives charged with the responsibility of converting prospects into loyal customers, the urge to tell all that you know can feel so right.

There is a widely-accepted notion in sales that, expertise trumps curiosity. Whether it is born out of confidence or insecurity, we have this compelling drive to tell customers all that we have, and all that we can do, instead of taking a more inquisitive approach and listening intently for the opportunity to say…

That's interesting; can you tell me more about that?

But as unnatural and counter-productive as this approach may seem, the research indicates that customers want to know how much you care before they care how much you know. Studies such as the Trust Project at Northwestern University and the work of respected researchers, Amy Cuddy and Susan Fisk, demonstrates that people give more weight to warmth over competence when making judgments on someone's trustworthiness.

For corporate leaders, Cuddy and company concluded in an article published in the Harvard Business Review that it is better to, "Connect, Then Lead."

And the bridge we travel over to earn the trust and form a deep personal relationship with the person sitting across the table is the connection of empathetic listening.

Tell me more about yourself.
Tell me more about what you're thinking.

We need to strip away all of the complexity that is inherent in today's sales cycle and get it down to its essential human quality, which is focusing on the client.

It is the responsibility of every sales executive to understand what problem the client is trying to solve. That can be done more thoroughly by diving deeper for more knowledge about the client's customers.

This entity is the one stakeholder that everyone should care about because they ultimately are the people who drive and generate value.

What the customer cares about
should be the focus.

Use this information to stop selling for a moment. Start a different kind of conversation and begin to build a deeper relationship with the client.

It needs to be a very genuine conversation on something the client cares about, instead of talking only about your products and services.

Traveling down this less-popular path where curiosity leads the way and expertise will bring up the rear, we offer some helpful prompts to make the journey less stressful:

Seek out the four curiosity prompts.

- Look for **surprises**. What comes across as unexpected or atypical?
- Identify where the customer places **value**, and has it changed since you saw them last?
- Search for **hacks** the client may be using. Are people improvising to make the system work?
- Uncover any **inconsistencies**. Is the customer saying one thing, but doing another?

In seemingly every interaction, one or more of these curiosity prompts are present, but are often obscured by our agenda.

It is important to note that curiosity prompts are not designed to close deals more quickly. They are to hone your senses to make you a better problem finder, and increase the likelihood that you will discover even more issues.

When we know our client's business as well, or better than they do, is when we will start to have more meaningful conversations. That is when we will be able to begin building a deeper rapport with our customers.

So on your next presentation, make a conscious effort to ask one more, **'tell me more.'** Remember the abundance and rewards that we seek are in the solutions we can deliver to our clients.

About Ashley Welch

Ashley is the Co-Founder of Somersault Innovation, a Design Thinking consulting firm which provides a unique approach to sales development and consulting services to companies such as Salesforce, Facebook, Microsoft, Forrester Research, Merck, Ellie Mae and others. (Design Thinking helps sales professionals stay customer centric and curious which leads to bigger opportunities!)

She and her co-founder, Justin Jones, wrote the book, *Naked Sales, How Design Thinking Reveals Customer Motives and Drives Revenue*. The book features customer success stories and tools from their Sell by Design program which is a learning process for sales team. Every team they have worked with has achieved a 100% or more gain in pipeline, followed by a substantial increase in revenue.

 Prior to founding Somersault Innovation, she spent the last twenty years as a leading sales professional, managing a multi-million dollar portfolio of global clients for a consulting firm. She has a strong wanderlust and loves to travel with her family. Closer to home, she founded and co-lead TEDxYouth@Wayland enabling students to tell their stories, spread inspiring ideas, and infuse the town with energy and activism.

Ashley's Recommendations

Read One Book
Change By Design by Tim Brown
How design thinking transforms organizations and inspires innovation.

Visit One Website
http://bit.ly/AshleysWebsite
This is a video, but is funny and clever. We should all take ourselves a little less seriously.

Subscribe to One Podcast
Revisionist History by Malcolm Gladwell
This podcast is a journey about the overlooked and misunderstood. Every episode re-examines something from the past - an event, a person, an idea, - and asks whether we got it right the first time.

19

"Thought awareness is the currency for overcoming limitations."

Thomas M. Sterner
Founder & CEO
The Practicing Mind Institute

If you reverse engineer any case study of personal fulfillment or professional prosperity, absent the rare mega-million lottery winning moments and other atypical lightening caught-in-a-bottle occurrences, the power source for success is rooted in the self-discipline to master your thoughts.

Noted self-help author, Napoleon Hill, wrote in his top-ten selling book of all-time, Think and Grow Rich, *"if you don't control what you think, you can't control what you do."*

And what was written more than 70 years ago holds true today. The mind will create thoughts with or without your permission, and it can be your master or your servant. Thought awareness offers you the opportunity to make that choice.

You cannot control what you are not aware of.

Now, most of our thoughts are not initiated by the real you. In fact, modern psychology states that about 95% of the thoughts we experience are actually reactions that are installed in our subconscious and merely firing off externally as we see different circumstances.

So even when we feel we are conscious in our thought process or decision making, the reality is we are more of a puppet to our subconscious. The goal of unlocking our boundless potential lies in beginning to shift some of the heavily stacked subconscious weight over to the Present Moment Functioning side of the scale.

In order to be fully present in each moment, you must strengthen the connection to **the observer within you** through thought awareness training. You must learn to operate from the perspective that you are not your thoughts, but rather you are the one who experiences your thoughts. Some thoughts you create intentionally, but most of us in large part are the victims of the thoughts our mind creates without our permission.

According to the National Science Foundation,

**The average person has between
12,000 and 60,000 thoughts per day.**

Of those daily mental messages, 80% are negative.

Without thought awareness, we cannot reverse the surreptitiously self-defeating mind talk that sabotages our best intentions and greatly limits our opportunity for meaningful personal growth.

By developing thought awareness, we give ourselves an empowering gift which is freedom of choice. This allows us to be a conscious choice maker.

**Meditation teaches us to be an observer of,
not a participant in, our thoughts.**

As individuals, we strengthen the ability to become more aware of our thoughts by one exercise that is commonly referred to as **meditation**. Through this practice we develop the ability to choose thoughts that are productive -- and lessen the ones that are not. In meditation, our thinking slows down and is much more purposeful. This creates the stage for our clarity to increase and our anxiety to diminish.

Meditation also cultivates a connection with **the observer,** which is who we really are, and not the fear-based power-hungry ego that we often unconsciously identify ourselves. As we become more connected with this observer, we are growing our thought awareness, and our ability to watch our thoughts instead of simply being immersed in them and reacting to whatever emotion or sensation they elicit.

There are two types of **meditative practices** you can try for 10-15 minutes, once or twice daily:

Breath-Based

Assume a comfortable position (sitting in a chair or cross-legged on the floor, or kneeling) and simply observe your body breathing.

Phrase-Based

Assume a comfortable position and choose a simple phrase to repeat. The phrase is likely best kept to three words or fewer and should be something that is soothing to you (i.e. *"I am still;"* *"I am quiet."*)

These two practices are deceptively simple exercises, but in the beginning each can be a low-key tug of war between your conscious and subconscious mind to lay claim to just who will control your thoughts. When you become aware that your mind has run off in a different direction instead of monitoring your breathing or your phrase/mantra, you simply bring it back into the present moment and the task at hand.

The quiet mind serves as a rudder to steer our efforts, and as awareness of our thoughts increases, the opportunity to choose how we experience each present moment also increases!

About Thomas Sterner

Thomas M. Sterner is the founder and CEO of The Practicing Mind Institute. As a successful entrepreneur he is considered an expert in Present Moment Functioning or PMF. He is a popular and in demand speaker who works with high performance individuals including athletes, coaches, industry groups, CEO's and individuals of all ages freeing them to operate effectively within high stress situations so that they can break through to new levels of mastery.

He is the author of the international best seller, *The Practicing Mind; Developing Focus and Discipline in Your Life* (New World Library 2012) and *Fully Engaged; Using The Practicing Mind In Daily Life* (New World Library 2016)

Prior to founding The Practicing Mind Institute he served as the Chief Concert Piano technician for a major performing arts center preparing instruments for the most demanding performances. During his 25 year tenure as a high level technician he personally worked for industry giants such as Van Cliburn, Pavarotti, Andre Watts, Ray Charles, Fleetwood Mac, Bonnie Raitt, Tony Bennett, Wynton Marsalis and many more. This provided the unique opportunity to converse with very noted disciplined minds on how they approached the process of "practicing" and dealing with stress when they needed to perform at the highest level.

Additionally Tom has worked with all ages and levels of golfers and his books have been read and recommended by touring pros. In his down time he is an accomplished musician, private pilot, experienced and avid golfer, sailor and target archer.

Thomas' Recommendations

Read One Book
Mastery, The Keys To success & Long Term Fulfillment
by George Leonard
This book shows how the process of mastery can help us attain a higher level of excellence and a deeper sense of satisfaction in our daily lives.

Visit One Website
SeanStephenson.com
Despite Dr. Sean Stephenson's medical challenges due to a rare bone disorder, the man often referred to as, "The three-foot giant," took a stand for a quality of life that has inspired millions.

Subscribe to One Podcast
TheLifeCoachSchool.com/podcasts
Master instructor, Brooke Castillo, teaches you how to teach yourself to use your mind to make your dreams come true.

20

"Be defined by what you love."

Ryan Hawk
Leadership Advisor
Brixey & Meyer

Founder and Host
The Learning Leader Podcast

There is no shortage of places where you can congregate with the masses, either in person or on some social media platform, to express your outrage and indignation over some perceived slight or misdeed that has occurred in any corner of your world.

But if you want to make a meaningful difference on a particular issue, and feel better while doing it, then separate yourself from the perpetually perturbed and lead with what you love.

There is no better time than today to lead with a positive attitude and advocate for the people and projects that are doing great work and accomplishing great things.

Don't be known for what you oppose.

There is no downside to having a positive mindset. Clearly, there is no guarantee that an upbeat attitude will deliver all of your personal and professional goals, but it will never be an impediment to success or identified as the root of any problem.

And the benefits of leading with positivity and choosing to look for the bright side of everything are practically immeasurable.

Your Health Is Better

There is evidence, hard and anecdotal, that people with a positive attitude are healthier because of a strong desire to take better care of themselves, and therefore live longer and more fulfilling lives.

Your Relationships Are Better

People naturally gravitate to those with a positive approach to life. Rare is the person who enjoys being around someone who focuses on the dark cloud instead of the silver lining.

Your Career Is Better

Success, more often than not, will be a strong validation for a positive attitude. It is indeed possible to achieve wealth and status with a mean and selfish spirit, but these lofty accomplishments rarely change this sour and suspicious approach to life. Success is possible on either path, but one is certainly more enjoyable.

Focusing on what you love leaves little time to feed and nourish the people and issues that annoy, disappoint or anger you. This mindset will lead these annoyances to inevitably wither and die in your life.

And the action steps to leading with what you love are as easy to implement as they are rewarding to embrace.

Practice Gratitude Daily

Make a conscious effort to sincerely thank the people who provide some level of service or comfort to you or your family as you go through the day. Not a comment or action that could be misconstrued as a gratuitous gesture or condescending air; just a simple, straightforward gesture of appreciation that soon will become second nature.

The only thing to do behind someone's back is to pat it!

The Write Way

Lead with what you love by expressing your appreciation to the authors and artists of work you admire. Challenge yourself to acknowledge the efforts of at least two people a day; either with an old-fashioned handwritten note or a shout-out on your favorite social media platform. This no-strings-attached, sincere gesture will set you apart from the pack of general sycophants or nay-sayers making the most noise in the public square, and give you a measure of satisfaction that it may be just what the recipient needs at this moment in their life.

Positive Gossip

If you find yourself in casual, unconstrained conversation with a small group of people, make sure your contributions to the tone of the talk is long on what you know and short on what you have heard. And make all of it positive.

Critique Buffers

Even in the most positive setting, there are times when a complaint or criticism needs to be leveled. When this situation arises, it is easier to remain calm when you begin the conversation with a compliment about the work or service done up to this point. This approach will keep the person on the receiving end of the critique from taking a defensive attitude and be more ready to accept and remedy the situation.

So make a determined effort to believe that a bright outlook is the right outlook and you will undoubtedly see and feel your life change for the better in all phases.

About Ryan Hawk

Ryan Hawk runs the Leadership Advisory team at Brixey & Meyer. Ryan has been a student, teacher, and practitioner of leadership and performance excellence most of his life.

First, as a collegiate and professional quarterback, and now in the business world. He shares what he's learned from his own experience as well as from interviewing more than 275 of the most thoughtful leaders in the world on his hit podcast, The Learning Leader Show. Ryan is a sought-after public speaker, an accomplished writer, and a trusted advisor to leaders all over the world.

The Learning Leader Show, is a top rated podcast that focuses on learning from the smartest, most creative leaders in the world (including such luminaries as Simon Sinek, Seth Godin, Kat Cole and Adam Grant). Hawk's podcast has exploded on a global scale with millions of listeners world-wide. Forbes has called The Learning Leader Show "The most dynamic leadership podcast out there." Inc. Magazine listed The Learning Leader Show as one of the top 5 podcasts to "help you lead smarter."

Ryan's Recommendations

Read One Book
The Wright Brothers by David McCullough
The dramatic story-behind-the-story about the courageous brothers who taught the world how to fly.

Visit One Website
WaitButWhy.com
Tim Urban and Andrew Finn's blog with over 600,000+ subscribers answering the question, why.

Subscribe to One Podcast
Dan Carlin's Hardcore History (DanCarlin.com)
Whether he is discussing history or current events, veteran journalist Dan Carlin brings his own unconventional approach to the subject matter.

21

"Developing a culture of accountability, starts with YOUR cadence."

Anthony Iannarino
Author & Sales Strategist

In the competitive world of Track and Field, successful hurdlers know the importance of establishing a winning cadence and rhythm in their race efforts. When a hurdler's cadence or stride is off, they are in serious trouble and likely poised for failure.

The same can be said for sales executives to become a more effective leader.

Establish a precise cadence within your organization.

There is a rhythm to business. Understanding that rhythm and working to ensure the proper cadence is critical to growing your sales organization.

There are three components that image-of-difference sales leaders need to discuss in detail with their sales team (or themselves) every week.

1) Gain a firm understanding of what's in the pipeline.
2) Know where the opportunities for growth are.
3) Conduct a weekly team gathering assessment.

Let's drill down on these three pacing principles.

The Pipeline Review

This is the foundation of establishing a good cadence, both individually and organizationally. Reviewing the pipeline to inspect how many new opportunities the team created in the prior week is the activity that ensures you have the ability to reach revenue goals. Without the right number of opportunities, you throw your future into doubt.

The pipeline session also allows you to inspect the overall health and viability of the opportunities in your funnel, ensuring they are progressing smoothly from target to close.

Without this personal self-scouting or team review, you will always be surprised, and most of these revelations will likely not be pleasant ones.

The Opportunity Review

This is the second rhythm regulator and teaching moment. Opportunity reviews are important blocks of time set aside to carefully examine if the prospect is truly viable. This process will help determine if you can create value for this dream client and that the team can formulate a winning game plan to be their new and potentially best, 'partner in profit.'

Opportunity reviews allow you to focus on strategy. It gives you the chance to explore questions such as, *"what is compelling this prospect to change?* And, *"how are we different, and how does that make a difference for this prospective customer?"*

Be cautious against falling into the trap of intermingling Pipeline and Opportunity reviews.

Quite often pipeline reviews wind up being opportunity reviews, and these two activities are different and need to be performed and completed separately. If you do not, the team may lose focus on prospecting which is necessary for ensuring a solid future pipeline review.

Team Huddles

And the last link in this critical chain of cadence is the huddle.

Make sure to improve from week to week; from month to month; and from quarter to quarter. Team Huddles provide a group setting format to deal with the challenges that you, or your sales force, will undoubtedly experience. This is a great way to share best practices; to brainstorm on how to overcome common obstacles; and to raise the team up by sharing successful strategies across the entire sales force.

Find ways to make sure team huddles are measured for their quality, and not their quantity.

Team Huddle meetings do not have to be long, but they must provide the people involved with actionable insights to be better immediately. Managed effectively, team huddles are a worthwhile investment of time and energy.

Embracing the concept of fine-tuning your business rhythm and cadence will allow successful leaders to clear each sales challenge with the precision of a world-class hurdler and elevate performance as a sales leader or account manager.

About Anthony Iannarino

Anthony is a widely-respected international speaker, author and sales leader.

He is a USA Today and Amazon best-selling author and has three books, *The Only Sales Guide You'll Ever Need; The Art of Closing -- Winning The Ten Commitments That Drive Sales;* and his newest book, *Eat Their Lunch -- Winning Customers Away From Your Competition.*

Mr. Iannarino's blog, www.thesalesblog.com attracts an average of 50,000 readers every month.

You can follow Anthony Iannarino on Twitter (@iannarino) and on Facebook.

Anthony's Recommendations

Read One Book
Antifragile: Things That Gain From Disorder
by Nassim Nicholas Taleb
This book is an investigation of luck, uncertainty, probability, risk, and decision-making in a world we don't understand.

Visit One Website
BrainPickings.org
An inventory of cross-disciplinary of interesting topics, spanning art, science, design, history, philosophy, and more.

Subscribe to One Podcast
Under The Skin with Russell Brand
A podcast hosted by the comedian and actor that asks the question, *"what's beneath the surface of the people, of the ideas that define our time, and of the history we are told."*

22

"Learn which feedback to ignore."

Jen Forman
Founder & CEO
Charlotte's Closet

We know that consumer feedback can be an important and accurate gauge to monitor corporate progress and to help plot the course for product innovation.

But not all comments from customers should be given equal weight and some feedback should be given little or no consideration when making critical business decisions.

Henry Ford, an American titan of industry and the founder of the Ford Motor Company famously stated, *"If I had asked people what they wanted, they would have said faster horses."* And every coach of a high-profile sports program knows that if they take too much advice from the fans sitting in the stands, one day they will likely find themselves sitting right alongside them!

Watch out for faulty feedback filters.

The ability to process both praise and criticism while extracting feedback that should be given a closer look (vs. discard) is vital to the growth of your business. A faulty feedback filter will soon leave you and your company buried under an avalanche of conflicting information with no clear understanding of how to dig out and get moving again.

Operating a business is the daily equivalent of running an obstacle course of challenges with you the owner or valued employee determined to clear or avoid the hurdles of varying levels of difficulty that you will encounter.

There will be no shortage of advice available for you to:

- Improve your product or service.
- Measure your customer's level of satisfaction.
- Demonstrate that you value your customer's opinion.
- Enhance your customer's experience with your product or service.

- Improve your ability to retain your customers.
- Make more informed business decisions.

All of this information and feedback is swirling around you and available for the asking.

The success-defining question is -- **how do you separate the wheat from the chaff** -- with all of this feedback at your fingertips?

Feedback from informed and helpful people is invaluable.

Dorie Clark, a marketing strategy consultant, author of several bestselling books, and an adjunct professor at Duke University's Fuqua Business School of Business wrote in the Harvard Business Review that she tried not to listen to feedback and found most of it, "either useless or destructive."

Clark offers several clear **"dismiss tips"** on how to accurately assess which well-intended feedback needs to be quickly discarded:

Dismiss Vague Feedback
If a person cannot tell you specifically what their complaint is (i.e., *"there is something not right." "It needs to be stronger,* etc.). It is not your job to figure out their criticism (unless they are your boss!)

Dismiss Singular Snubs
If one customer delivers a fairly negative critique, you should not give it much weight. The opinion of one person, no matter how influential the person, is rarely reliable. However, if one

sour note cascades into a steady stream of bad reviews, you would be wise to listen.

Dismiss Digs On Things That Work
If you are targeting a specific market with your product and you receive negative feedback from outside of that niche demographic, then you are on the right path with this "addition by subtraction" critique.

Dismiss Suspect Sources
Decide in advance who you respect and only choose to listen to those trusted peers, colleagues, and credible sources. The rest of the fast-flowing feedback should pass swiftly through your filter.

Dismiss Personal Put Downs
Perhaps we are becoming a less-civil society, as people seem more emboldened to share their hurtful but 'honest' feedback face-to-face. And the anonymity of the Internet provides a wider passage for snarky comments to reach you. But to ignore this mean-spirited feedback is sound advice. If it has any legitimacy, it will eventually come to you from a respected source or a trusted person.

Without question, feedback is important for your career or business to survive and thrive. But so is the ability to discern what advice to take and act on. Without it, you could soon find yourself embracing that 'faster horse' concept Mr. Ford so skillfully avoided!

About Jen Forman

Jen spent her professional career as a media director at a mid-size PR firm where she was instrumental in securing national and local media placements on behalf of her lifestyle clients.

Seeing a void in shopping options for her own daughter, she took her expertise to launch Charlotte's Closet, where she booked herself to talk teen fashion trends and ways to save during prom season on both national and local morning shows to introduce brand and rental concept.

Charlotte's Closet has been featured on a number of media outlets including, *The Today Show, CNN, Good Day New York, WNBC-NY, Great Day Houston, Good Morning Texas* and *Twin Cities Live.*

Charlotte's Closet is disrupting online shopping for Gen Z by providing access to borrow designer dresses for all events at up to 75% off retail. This retailer is first to market in the teen rental space and offers its young clients exclusive shopping experiences including a home try on service. The brand currently ships trendy fashions to teens in 48 states.

Jen's Recommendations

Read One Book
Girl, Stop Apologizing by Rachel Hollis
Who you are is defined by the next decision you make, not the last one. The author of this book urges women to stop apologizing for their hopes, desires and dreams and instead to go after them with confidence.

Visit One Website
CookingLight.com
A website to help you make smart choices for a healthy lifestyle.

Subscribe To One Podcast
"How I Built This" by Guy Raz
This podcast weaves the narrative journey about innovators, entrepreneurs, and idealists --- along with the movements they built.

23

"Give advice, not answers."

Will Anastas
Senior Vice President of Sales,
Procore Technologies

There is the familiar ancient Chinese proverb that suggests giving a man a fish and you will feed him for a day, but teach a man to fish and you feed him for a lifetime. This offers a timeless reminder on the short-term benefits of serving up an answer to a coworker's problem compared to providing sound advice that will teach them how to solve a particular issue, as well as a lifetime of other challenges.

The successful sales leaders and sought-after mentors are the ones that guide their people through a process of arriving at a decision themselves, as opposed to simply serving up the answer to the dilemma of the day.

The rhythmic give-and-take cadence in the art of offering advice looks natural and easy with a skilled advisor at the wheel and an eager listener with good intentions on the other end. But good counsel is far from an off-the-cuff exercise in guiding the seeker to the solution to their problem.

When the advice process is done well, both sides benefit.

When the advisor and seeker are truly connected, both come away better from the experience. The recipient learns one or more solutions to fix today's and tomorrow's problems, and the advisor strengthens a relationship with the recipient who undoubtedly feels a measure of gratitude and indebtedness.

Those accepting the mantle of providing sound advice to struggling seekers face a host of challenges as they try to assess the depth of the stated problem, and also carefully probe to reveal any unstated barriers that are standing in the way of a workable remedy.

Subordinates or colleagues often come in the guise of being an advice seeker, but they are only looking for validation of the decision they have already made. Other reasons could be they are surreptitiously soliciting praise from their superior, or they want to spread the risk by bringing management into the final decision to diminish the personal fallout on a less than favorable outcome.

Seeking and giving advice can be the integral fuel additive that boosts the effectiveness of an organization's talent pool and management team.

A skilled advisor can span the range of providing specific feedback to a single problem, or to dive deeper and offer when asked, counseling to address a more complex problem. Further involvement could be coaching and mentoring an advice seeker looking earnestly for career development.

Some tactical advice on how to maximize your time and effort when stepping into the advisory arena would be to consider:

Know Your Limits

Turn up your self-awareness radar to recognize if your unsolicited advice is being accepted in the spirit that it is being offered, and are you qualified to speak on the topic you are choosing to weigh in on.

It Is Not About You

Framing your advice with personal experiences does not bring the level of empathy and consideration that the situation warrants and the seeker deserves. Respect the recipient's overall skills and their status on the corporate ladder.

Measure Twice, Cut Once

Collect the necessary data to gain a firm understanding of the problem to be solved. Refrain from a snap judgment that the problem is similar to another issue you have solved. Ask ego-free questions to be sure you have all of the pertinent facts.

No Strings Attached Advice

Convey to the seeker they are free to accept or modify your counsel without any offense taken. Pure advice is ego-free and void of any resentment. Implied conditions will stifle the growth of the seeker and the effectiveness of the advisor.

Communicate Clear, Concise Counsel

Avoid vague and nebulous recommendations that can lead to the seekers misunderstanding of the advice. When providing suggestions that are of a technical or specialized nature, be certain you are speaking at the seeker's level of proficiency.

Being sought out for advice is a trusted responsibility, so don't be the counselor who serves up a "one fish" solution to a problem, but rather be the advisor who teaches the seeker how to fish to ensure long-term success!

About Will Anastas

Will serves as the Senior Vice President of Sales at Procore Technologies. He is responsible for building strategic partnerships with companies looking to change the way they approach customer service.

His sales leadership extends beyond building pipeline and closing deals, and into looking for true synergies with customers, as well as building and mentoring the sales team with that goal in mind. He most recently spent the last seven years as Senior Vice President of Enterprise Corporate Sales for Salesforce, where he also led their North American Business Development team. At Salesforce, he and his team were tasked with building new customer relationships, as "hunters," and expanding the new customers across the Salesforce platform.

Will has over 23 years of experience as an established thought leader in all things sales. He has written extensively about his experience and vision for the future of sales, and served as a featured speaker at Dreamforce. When not at work, Will spends his time with his wife, and two wonderful children.

Will's Recommendations

Read One Book
Daring Greatly: How The Courage To Be Vulnerable Transforms The Way We Live, Love, Parent and Lead
by Brene Brown
Thought leaders Brene Brown explains how vulnerability is both the core of difficult emotions like fear and disappointment, and the birthplace of love, belonging, innovation and creativity.

Visit One Website
Procore.com
Experience the world's most widely used construction platform.

Subscribe to One Podcast
Quotable (The Podcast) -- Quotable.com
A contributor-driven site offering advice and guidance designed to inspire and empower modern sales, service, and marketing leaders and those that support them. Explore hundreds of insightful and actionable articles and podcasts on sales, marketing, customer success, business strategy, finance, leadership, and much more.

24

"Forget your strategy. Focus on the customer's strategy."

Anthony Reynolds
Chief Executive Officer
Altify

In his 1961 inaugural address, President John F. Kennedy spoke his famous challenging words, *"Ask not what your country can do for you, ask what you can do for your country."* And today some six decades later, sales professionals should embrace this wise counsel and, ask not what your customers can do for you, ask what you can do for your customers.

While there has always been a degree of complexity in business-to-business selling, the proliferation of information and connectedness among people has created a far more sophisticated buyer with newly-cultivated high expectations.

Buyers have access to a wealth of data that allows them to make informed purchases, and this dawning insight requires a different approach to selling.

Put the customer at the center of everything you do.

The only way to sustainably grow revenue is to have a relentless focus on the customer. The Altify 2019 Customer Revenue Optimization Benchmark study validates the thirst for revenue growth is the top business priority for 89% of the companies polled, followed closely (87%) by the concern for customer retention.

Both of these concerns can be better met by resisting the temptation to come in selling to your customer, but instead, focus on gaining a clear understanding of their concerns and problems and how they are trying to deal with them.

The old world order of business - what can you do for me - is viewed as transactional; whereas the new world order – what can you do for others – focuses on building trusting relationships by taking a sincere interest in the customer's needs. The old world fixates on price and limits interest to the direct buyers. While the new world emphasizes value, return on investment and looks to build quality relationships throughout the organization.

In reality, there are two core tenants to everything we do in business – people and problems. People are the dynamics of our relationships and the political influencers that are a part of every decision. Problems center on the customer's current dilemma that trusted advisors closely study to uncover the initiatives created and the resources allocated to solve them. True advisors resist presenting a commercial solution until the appropriate situation and time.

Insight mapping creates a path to be a partner in profit with the customer.

We are witnessing a whole new category emerging called Customer Revenue Optimization (CRO). This paradigm-shifting practice places the customer at the center and enlists every employee to be a meaningful contributor to the revenue team.

This approach is best understood in how you optimize the revenue of your customers. This can only occur when you truly understand their business - including the revenue drivers of the company. It is an introduction to a new science of selling where software meets methodology that is guided by artificial and augmented intelligence. But at the heart of this is the seller's desire to truly empathize and walk in the shoes of their stakeholders and understand what keeps them up at night.

Strongly consider embracing the following tactics to provide a smooth transition out of the old world of sales and into more rewarding account relationships:

Map Your Thoughts

Document your customer's goals, objectives, and key results into whatever Customer Relationship Management (CRM) system your company uses. It is imperative all selling teams can share in researching and collaborating to build this powerful customer insight.

Use Visualization Tools

Whether your choice is a basic PowerPoint presentation or a more CRM integrated tool (like the Altify Insight Map), invest the time to draw it out. Creating a simple visual that offers a clear vision of your connection between corporate goals and how to overcome business pressure are table stakes for becoming a trusted advisor.

Share Your Plan

Print the detailed action plan of your goals and tactics to share with your customer. This will confirm the strategy or present an opportunity to edit the plan, either way deepening and strengthening your relationship.

The dawn is breaking on a new world order of professional selling and it lies in asking not what your customer can do for you, but in asking what you can do for your customer!

About Anthony Reynolds

Anthony is the Chief Executive Officer of Altify. Altify is the Customer Revenue Optimization company, helping businesses generate value and grow revenue.

Providing best practices, methodology and technology, Altify helps revenue teams visualize customers and their desired outcomes, unlocking revenue growth and building sales excellence.

Prior to Altify, Anthony was the Executive Vice President and Chief Customer Officer at Anaplan (NYSE: PLAN) when the company grew from 250 to 650 employees. He also served as a General Manager and senior executive at SAP (NYSE: SAP) and Business Objects.

He holds an MBA from the University of Cambridge in England and a Bachelor of Commerce and Business Administration from the University of British Columbia in Canada. Anthony is on the Board of the Los Gatos and Saratoga Recreation and resides in Los Gatos, California. Anthony is married with two children.

Anthony's Recommendations

Read One Book
Leaders Eat Last: Why Some Teams Pull Together, And Others Don't
by Simon Sinek
In this bestseller, Simon Sinek challenges assumptions about how and why people seek accept inspiration from significant leaders and organizations.

Visit One Website
SeekingAlpha.com
A great place to get up to date info on companies and potential customers.

Subscribe to One Podcast
Revenue Optimization Radio, hosted by Patrick Morrissey
RevenueOptimizationRadio.com
(or wherever you subscribe to podcasts)
This podcast talks to the top B2B sales leaders, sales ops, enablement and marketing execs to help you crack the code to high performance selling.

25

"Focus on the art of creating commitments with people."

Mike Horrey
Founder and CEO
Neat Tucks

Commitment is the critical component in every successful relationship that transforms the promises made to each other into reality.

Whether on the front lines selling a product or leading those responsible for securing market share, the prosperity of both duties comes through commitment.

The only way for someone to really gauge how effective they are being in a presentation is to look at things *the buyer* (i.e. client/prospect or subordinate) is going to do. Sadly, all too often a sales professionals mistakenly proceed with, *'I'll do this, and this, and this, etc.'* Then hope they will be able to get what is wanted at the end.

When in reality it has to be, *'I'll do this, the client or staffer does this, and then we move forward. I'll do this and the client or staffer does this, and we move forward, etc.'*

When a salesperson chooses to dump everything they have on the table and wait until the end to engage the buyer in negotiating this deal; the give and take will undoubtedly take place in the muck and mire of pushing for price reductions and better terms.

See each stage of a needed buyer's commitment as a "toll booth" moment.

However if in this process, the sales leader or executive can view the commitment stages they are looking from the buyer's side as "toll booth" moments – a point of mutual exchanges – then the journey stands to be a more rewarding one for both parties.

Every sales performance is about creating an experience for the customer, and then the buyer does something as a result. And if a sales executive can focus on the experiences they are creating, *and then* on the commitments they are looking for the buyer to make and keep, then change will happen fast.

While appearances can be deceiving, and what looks and feels like a productive and constructive conversation from both vantage points, can turn out to be all sizzle and no substance.

Reality

Conversations do not lead to successful performances in sales or in coaching. It is a commitment, or lack thereof, that determines results.

The shorter the learning curve on this important lesson, the faster that success will be the outcome in most of the undertaken tasks.

Focus on the art of creating commitments with people.

Whether it is selling to a client/prospect, or coaching a sales representative, a clear understanding is needed on what the commitments are at each "toll booth" stage of the process.

The ability to deliver on this clear understanding is what will ultimately separate the pretenders from the contenders.

Being aptly prepared with sharpened intuitive talent and packed with the necessary technology tools will remove all of the mystery from every presentation. Delivering predictable results based detailed executions is the goal and the likely outcome.

We are designed to help customers make and keep commitments, and then measure the responsiveness to the change that occurs.

And that starts with a sales review of what activities need to happen to be successful, and what skills are required to accomplish this.

- For **every stage,** there should be specific activities outlined.
- For **every activity**, there will be specific skills required.
- For **every skill,** there must be supportive corporate resources.

Experience and research have revealed that people are generally proficient at tracking the sales stages and some of the key activities. But many fall down in the areas of tracking the things that we want – those toll booth moments.

Image of difference performers will be aware of the things they need to happen in order to really know they are going to have the right commitment made and kept.

You will dramatically increase the chances of achieving the desired results from the person on the other side of the negotiation table when you take them down the road while passing through the commitment "toll booths" you have constructed.

About Mike Horrey

Michael Horrey is an entrepreneur, creator of Neat Tucks, and an inspired mentor to other business owners. He believes in combining faith, calculated personal growth and prior experiences to realize one's maximum potential in business.

Previously, he made his mark as a management leader at AT&T where he earned the company's top individual honor — the Circle of Excellence Award — twice. This experience, coupled with achieving proficiency in web development as well as learning garment and manufacturing industry skills have been instrumental in his career after his time in corporate America.

Michael knows the true way to grind with purpose is to work with -- and within your passion. In creating Neat Tucks, "the best way to keep your shirt tucked in," Michael came up with his own prototypes and learned the requisite skills to bring his vision to fruition. His drive earned him the chance to meet valuable mentors and gather strategic advice from the likes of Daymond John of FUBU and Shark Tank to further develop his brand.

Michael encourages people to try different learning methods to see what is most effective for them. Harnessing past experience and participation in various certification programs, small business development centers, social media, online courses and

YouTube are methods Michael endorses for the modern entrepreneur to foster continued personal growth.

 Michael attributes his drive and purpose to his favorite team: his wife and two sons.

Mike's Recommendations

Read One Book
Rich Dad- Poor Dad by Robert Kiyosoki
The #1 Personal Finance book of all time. It's the story of his two dads: his real father, whom he calls his 'poor dad,' and the father of his best friend, the man who became his mentor and his 'rich dad.'

Visit One Website
DuctTapeMarketing.com
"Clever marketing ideas galore and lots of contrarian thinking on what works and what doesn't," says Forbes Magazine.

Subscribe to One Podcast
Business Wars on Apple iTunes or Stitcher.
Gives you the unauthorized, real story of what drives these companies and their leaders, inventors, investors and executives to new heights -- or to ruin. Hosted by David Brown, former anchor of Marketplace.

26

"Leave people better than you found them."

Beth Kaplan
Vice President,
Global Enablement & Strategic Programs
Medidata Solutions

Those who enjoy the great outdoors, communing with nature and sleeping under the stars will tell you the number one rule of camping is, *"to leave the campsite better than you found it."*

Now consider for a moment extending this camper's covenant to your professional relationships and focus on creating a working environment that allows a person to maximize their full potential.

By shifting your focus to a mindset of "getting to know your people and to grow your people," it will become abundantly clear the staggering amount of untapped employee talent that begins to flow forth and increase the company's operating efficiency.

Unskilled 'drillers' are at the core of the untapped talent problem.

The research is clear that people desperately want to be coached and will change jobs for the prospect of working with and for a visionary leader. But sadly, the managers tasked with this responsibility are dramatically ill-placed and unprepared.

A study conducted by Bridge, a Utah based employee development company, revealed that 67% of millennials would leave a job that lacked growth opportunities and failed to offer paths for leadership development.

And this quest for quality mentoring may seemingly be a search for the proverbial needle in a haystack. A Gallup study demonstrated that **companies fail to choose a management candidate with the right talent for the job a staggering 82% of the time.**

Furthermore, Gallup research estimates that managers account for at least 70% of the variance in employee engagement. With this combination of hiring the wrong leaders and their vast influence, it is not surprising that only 30% of U.S. employees are engaged at work. And that number plummets to a shockingly low 13% worldwide.

It is a universal longing of people to have leaders believe in them enough to develop them and forge this nurturing spirit with the requisite skill set to make it happen.

Building a thriving and fully-actualized workforce takes a sincere investment of time to understand the values and goals of each worker.

Where do you see yourself and how can I help get you there?

In her illuminating book, "Multipliers" author Liz Wiseman drives home the point that it is not how intelligent your team members are; but rather how you can draw out that intelligence to maximize the person's full potential.

Wiseman boldly classifies winning leaders as "multipliers" who consciously and skillfully get more effort, energy, and achievement from their staff. This type of leader's sincere enthusiasm generates a belief that the impossible is actually possible. This is in stark contrast to leaders who earn the label of a "diminisher" for routinely draining the energy from their group by constantly trying to prove *THEY* are the smartest person in the room. Here are three key focus areas for how you can leave people better than you found them.

Help Teams Build Their Own Professional Roadmap

Understanding where the person is starting from will require an inquisitive deep dive on your part to learn about the interests, skills, and motivation of the colleague. With this greater insight, together you will outline a path that will fuel the sustained motivation needed and to plot the right course for a rewarding and satisfying career.

Focus On Creating A High-Performance File

Help colleagues create a personal collection of key skills and accomplishments that leverages their superior talents and strengths. This also should deemphasize their weaknesses and shortcomings while shedding light into future development opportunities. Documenting this file will be a valuable tool for promotions and merit awards. Make sure to review it quarterly with your team members and use it as a roadmap to success.

Align Tasks To Strengths

This will lead to early success and breed the necessary confidence in the staffer to accept the challenge and responsibility of more complex assignments. As Liz Wiseman says, *"look for that 'native genius' in everyone."*

Developing people requires the courage of your own leadership skills and patience to deal with the failure that may arise from staffers heading into deeper waters. It is your role to ask the probing questions that allow the person to work through the obstacles and find their way to success.

Leaving people and campsites better than you found them is always the goal, but in the former, leaders should most definitely keep the fire burning!

About Beth Kaplan

Beth Kaplan Kondonijakos leads Global Sales Enablement and Leadership Development at Medidata Solutions. Prior to this, she started the Salesforce Sales Leader Enablement program, and is credited as a thought leader in this space.

Beth has over 15 years experience in training and leadership development and is a proven leader at reducing new hire ramp time and transforming learning culture by giving sales the knowledge and strategies needed to become selling all-stars. Beth has a Bachelor of Arts in English Writing/Rhetoric and Communications from the University of Pittsburgh. She is currently pursuing her doctorate at the University of Pennsylvania in leadership and learning strategy.

When she's not focused on making sales more productive, she enjoys giving back to her community through causes like the Make-A-Wish Foundation.

Beth's Recommendations

Read One Book
Multipliers by Liz Wiseman
This Wall Street Journal bestseller explores why some leaders drain capability and intelligence from their teams while others amplify it to produce better results.

Visit One Website
BreneBrown.com
This bestselling author and highly-rated speaker encourages everyone to own your life story and love yourself through the process.

Subscribe to One Podcast
WorkLife with Adam Grant
Organizational psychologist Adam Grant takes you inside the minds of some of the world's most unusual professionals to discover the keys to a better work life.

27

"Cultivate an uncompromisable commitment to integrity."

David Owens
Director, Camden County (NJ)
Dept. of Corrections and Juvenile Justice

The enigmatic but principled author, Harper Lee, who won the Pulitzer Prize for her first novel, To Kill A Mockingbird, had the following response to the loud public clamor for her decades-long hiatus from publishing another book:

> *"People are entitled to full respect for their opinions. But before I can live with other folks, I've got to live with myself. The only thing that doesn't abide by majority rule is a person's conscience."*

Integrity, no matter what the profession or circumstance, means having a moral compass set to do what is right; and having the inner strength and fortitude to do what is right.

It is the voice in your head that has been nurtured by guardians and mentors to do good, and to be a help to others, where and when you can.

Now undoubtedly in business, it takes a high level of skill and expertise in your chosen endeavor, along with an ability to network and connect with people to succeed. But there is another critical component that ties skill and personality together to sustain long-term success,

Doing what's right is not easy and can sometimes come at a high price.

Integrity and character are interchangeable terms that are the foundation of the Trinity for Success. It is what provides the catalyst for trust to take root and allow your skills and reworking relationships to grow.

People want to grow their business with employees and vendors they trust and respect. Owners quite often will go against their intuition and employ or buy from someone out of a perceived necessity. But their radar is always set to find and invest in the staffer or supplier who possesses the integrity to use their talents honestly and forthrightly to maximize the company's potential.

That the old adage of, *"honesty being the best policy"* remains true still today is underscored in Thomas J. Stanley's book, The Millionaire Mind. The author surveyed 733 millionaires and asked them to rank 30 factors which played a role in their good fortune and, **"being honest with all people" tied for the top ranking with, "being well disciplined."** The factor of being able to be trusted was prominently mentioned linked with, "getting along with people" which placed a close third on the list.

Curiously, "being lucky" and "graduating near or at the top of my class" ranked 27th and 30th, respectively on this millionaires Success Factor list.

So it is no wonder that integrity and success are the bookends that hold a lifetime of consistently honorable words and deeds. People with integrity are the image-of-difference employees and leaders that lift companies to great heights.

This sentiment was echoed by Nigerian novelist, Chinua Achebe, who succinctly stated...

One of the truest tests of integrity is its blunt refusal to be compromised.

Workers with integrity consistently give their best effort because of an internal commitment and not an external pressure or motive. And they do not pass blame when things go wrong, but will always share credit for a project well done.

Integrity is a muscle that must be exercised daily if it is to be strong enough to carry the weight of making hard decisions when easier, less ethical solutions present themselves.

Write What Is Your Right

Reflect on and commit to a personal mission statement that clearly articulates your values and sensibilities. This personal credo will offer guidance when confronted with a situation that will test your integrity.

Build Quality Relationships

Trust and respect are characteristics that flow both ways. They are often given more readily by others towards you; the more they are demonstrated by you towards others.

Lead By Example

Let your actions be guided by the words of Ralph Waldo Emerson who remarked, *"What you do speaks so loudly that I cannot hear what you say."*

Display Your Integrity Identity

Once you have an understanding of who you are, and who you want to become, begin to live your personal mission statement consistently. Make sure that your words and deeds are internally driven and not a script written by others that you are reluctantly following.

Remember, it is you alone that will cast the deciding majority rule vote on whether you will live a life with an uncompromisable commitment to integrity!

About David Owens

David Owens is a nationally respected law enforcement figure with a distinguished career that has spanned five decades in the Department of Corrections.

David began his career in law enforcement as a Corrections Officer for the Philadelphia Prison System in 1964 and rose through the ranks, holding every position in the chain of command. He worked in every institution in the Department and commanded the Pre-Release Program that received two national awards for outstanding programming.

In 1978 David was appointed Warden of Holmesburg Prison and the following year he was assigned to the Detention Center to bring that facility up to standards. He was soon appointed Superintendent of the Philadelphia Prisons, eventually becoming the first African American to hold the office of Commissioner of the Pennsylvania Department of Corrections.

During David Owens' administration, the Department opened two new state corrections facilities and began the planning for SCI Chester. The Department also increased its minority employees by eighteen percent.

In 1989, David resigned as commissioner of The Department of Corrections and returned to Philadelphia to establish the Owens Group, a criminal justice consultant firm.

But in 1993, the Freeholders of Camden County, NJ asked Owens to become Warden/ Director of the County's Department of Correction. Subsequently he was appointed Camden County Deputy County Administrator for Public Safety.

Retiring from public service after 41-years, David was appointed Interim Warden for CCDOC and Juvenile Justice, and eventually named the Director.

David's Recommendations

Read One Book

Leadership In The Bible – A Practical Guide For Today
By Paul Ohana and David Arnow
This book provides guidance about the most effective ways of responding to forty challenging situations you encounter every day. This guidance is grounded in the wisdom of three key figures in Hebrew Scripture -- Abraham, Joseph, and Moses.

Visit One Website

https://Drucker.Institute (that's right, .institute, not .com)
Founded to carry on the work of Mr. Peter Drucker, touted by Business Week magazine as, "the man who invented management." The mission of the Drucker Institute is to promote strengthening organizations in order to strengthen society.

28

"Make yourself indispensable."

John Gabriel
NBA Executive Advisor
Orlando Magic Basketball Club

It is a worthy goal and realistic idea to be a vitally important part of the success of any group endeavor. However, every day experiences prove to us that no one is truly indispensable.

Death, illness and injury have demonstrated countless times in the world of business, entertainment, and sports that, *'the show must go on.'* This requires the battle plan of the next person up to be implemented and the work continues.

So while a concession is made to the literal definition that no one is indispensable; there also is a less tangible truth that author, Ufuoma Apoki, points out:

Things are just not right when some people aren't around.

You need to source and sharpen the skills and habits that forge passion and purpose to earn the label of being highly-valued, and yes perhaps even touted as indispensable.

The landscape of the modern workplace has undergone seismic shifts, and leaders should identify the critical building material to shore up the employment ground beneath your feet.

Noted author Seth Godin reveals in his book, "Linchpin: Are You Indispensable?" that --

> *"The only way to get what you're worth is to stand out, to exert emotional labor, to be seen as indispensable, and to produce interactions that organizations and people care deeply about."*

With this ever-changing business environment, the challenge to be the best and not rest on your laurels is brought to everyone's doorstep. Sadly, some choose to ignore the specter of standing on status quo, and do so at their own peril.

However, those who embrace every opportunity to take on additional responsibilities that bring added value to the company will move closer to earning the nebulous label of being indispensable if there was a call for layoffs. And broadening your work lane in a way that enhances the productivity of your colleagues is also banking ample reasons to support a future request for a raise.

While no employee may be indispensable you can:

Bring an abundance of value that will make it difficult to replace.

If your goal is to move from 'good' to 'much better' and push closer to being categorized as 'difficult to replace' it is imperative individuals engage in the business equivalent of 'cross-training.'

The Harvard Business Review refers to this cross-training as strengthening complementary work skills as, **nonlinear development**.

For example, someone already considered technically adept, should focus on self-improvement training to build up their communication skills. This will make their technical expertise more apparent and accessible to coworkers and supervisors, while strengthening their position and value within the company.

Great leaders know there is little value in proclaiming your value when it pertains to organizational initiatives. The actions you take speak louder than anything you might say.
To that end, consider letting these additional actions make your case as a highly valued professional:

Be a Taskmaster

Step forward enthusiastically to secure the duties of an important corporate task. Look for opportunities for these responsibilities to arise when a coworker departs, or when the company expands and a new task is created.

Do Your Job, Plus

Perform your areas of responsibility at a high level of proficiency, but look to provide more insight and critical thought to assist the company with forecasting and new opportunities for growth.

Display Your Character

Demonstrate the traits that identify you as representing the company's stated culture. Consistently show with your words and deeds that you are trustworthy; reliable; a positive thinker; supportive of others and the company's goals; consistent and stable in temperament; and adaptable to change.

Have Dedication for Education

To be considered indispensable, you have to be viewed as a destination for information and insight by your colleagues and supervisor. This will require you to stay current with the latest industry news, technologies, and trends, and more importantly, the ability to understand how this information will impact you, your department, and the company.

While no one presumably can ever wear the crown of being truly indispensable; you certainly can work harder and smarter to earn all of the privileges and benefits that come with the indefinable title!

About John Gabriel

John Gabriel's fierce work ethic and humble servant's spirit has forged a distinguished career in the National Basketball Association that spans four decades and has earned him acclaim and respect throughout pro basketball around the world.

A creative intellect and versatile skill set was John's entrée into making a living at the game he played and starred in at Kutztown University. An entry-level position in the Philadelphia 76ers ticket office quickly expanded to be the team's video coordinator and the marketing department's production manager for all TV and radio commercials.

When the city of Orlando, Florida was awarded an NBA franchise, Gabriel was the team's first hire and was tabbed to help build the organization, on and off the court.

John's energy and attitude lifted him up the NBA ladder and his basketball prowess helped place the Magic in the post season 12 of his 15 years with the team. He was named the Magic's General Manager in 1996 and his efforts earned him NBA Executive of the Year honors in 2000.

Gabriel left the Magic in 2004 and spent the next 13 seasons contributing his basketball insight to the Portland Trailblazers and to Phil Jackson and the New York Knicks before returning to the Magic in 2017 in his current position as Executive Advisor.

In 2011, John was diagnosed with Parkinson's disease and once again he has channeled his time and talent with laser focus on another important personal goal. In recent years, John has helped raise more than $1 million for the Parkinson's Association of Central Florida.

John resides in Winter Park, Florida with his wife, Dorothy, and they enjoy the love and company of their three grown children.

John's Recommendations

Read One Book
The Power of Now - A Guide To Spiritual Enlightenment
by Eckhart Tolle
A word of mouth phenomenon since its first publication in 1997. The Power of Now is one of those rare books with the power to change the lives of the reader for the better.

Visit One Website
IHHP.com with Dr. J.P. Pawliw-Fry
Dr. Pawliw-Fry's offers research-based strategies to help people manage their emotions in stressful situations.

Subscribe to One Podcast
This Is Your Life with Michael Hyatt
With more than 14 million downloads, this podcast (under its new name, Lead To Win), combines research with groundbreaking strategies to help you win at work, succeed at life, and lead with confidence.

29

"Discover your productive passion."

Todd Henry
Founder
The Accidental Creative

A young Theodore Roosevelt harnessed a robust spirit to lift an often frail body to great heights and firmly believed the best prize life offered us all was **the chance to work hard at work worth doing.**

The great American statesman was galvanized and guided by a productive passion of wanting to improve the lives of everyday people, and his efforts delivered landmark social and political reform in the burgeoning United States.

Now, as you take this moment of personal reflection to explore where your true passions lie, it is important to understand the inherent paradox of the word itself.

The Latin derivation of the word passion is -- *pati* -- which means "to suffer or endure." The word, *compassion* embraces the meaning of "to suffer with."

So this is not a journey about discovering your passion by evaluating the requisite joy and pleasure derived from specific activities. It is quite the opposite. Productive passion is about defining the battles you are willing to fight to achieve the outcomes that you are deeply passionate about accomplishing.

Great work requires suffering for something beyond yourself.

And it is created when you bend your life around a mission and spend yourself on something you deem worthy of your best effort. Productive passion must be your compass if you want to avoid the lure of comfort and fear.

We understand that the problems encountered in the future will not be solved by half-hearted folks phoning it in. They will be remedied by people who have connected deeply to what drives them, along with building practices into their lives each day to help enact productive passion with peers, friends, family, and the world.

Can you lay your head down tonight satisfied with the work you did today?

The key to earning an affirmative answer to this nightly quest for peace of mind can only be found in your daily attitude, approach and your activities. You need to recognize the emotional patterns that trigger your productive passion and also sharpen your be-in-the-moment perspective. This critical combination will fuel the meaningful work that will serve more than your own needs.

Identify your igniters of passion.

Compassionate Anger
Look for the situations that have you feeling like -- *'somebody should do something about that!'* This is where your productive passion is brewed.

For Crying Out Loud
Passion can be found in the moments that move you to tears. Seeing people fight valiantly to overcome great obstacles may spark you to contribute your time and talent for a daunting but worthy cause. This is also where productive passion is born.

Hope Springs Eternal
And it is the circumstances of dire occasions where you can remain hopeful. Being able to create a favorable outcome when everyone else has written the matter off as a lost cause is where your productive passion resides.

Live Life As An Open Book

Now the question, 'What would you do if tomorrow was to be the last day of your life," will elicit answers that are both provocative and poignant.

But a more powerful exercise to consider is asking,

> "How would you act tomorrow if you knew you were going to be observed all day by someone taking detailed notes which would be turned into a book?"

Undoubtedly, most people would act differently in this stylized tomorrow knowing a snapshot of their thoughts, words, and deeds were to become the permanent testament of their life. This imagined best behavior of how you would prefer to define yourself is the catalyst. Here you can pull out of your comfort zone and do what you know is right.

When considering what it would be like to have your life on display, remember it is your actions and productive passions that ultimately define you, not your good intentions.

So shift your search from the tasks that will bring you joy, and fervently seek the best prize life can offer you – the opportunity to work hard at work worth doing!

About Todd Henry

Todd teaches leaders and organizations how to establish practices that lead to everyday brilliance.

He is the author of four books, *The Accidental Creative, Die Empty, Louder Than Words, and Herding Tigers,* which have been translated into more than a dozen languages, and he speaks and consults across dozens of industries on creativity, leadership, and passion for work.

His book, *Die Empty* was named by Amazon.com as one of the best books of 2013. His latest book, *Herding Tigers*, is about what creative people need from their leader, and how to give it to them.

Todd's Recommendations

Read One Book
Herding Tigers - Be The Leader Creative People Need
By Todd Henry
A practical handbook for every manager charged with leading teams to creative brilliance.

Visit One Website
AccidentalCreative.com
Explore concrete practices that will lead to sharper focus, improved productivity, and better collaboration.

Subscribe to One Podcast
ToddHenry.com/podcasts/
With millions of downloads, The Accidental Creative podcast has delivered weekly tips and ideas for staying prolific, brilliant, and healthy since 2005.

30

"Invest your time like money."

Elizabeth Grace Saunders
Founder & CEO
Real Life E

From our earliest years we have been taught, challenged and even warned about the impact of how we spend our time and our money. And as you got older, and finances became more plentiful, you were counseled on the importance of investing your expanding wealth for long-term benefits. But sadly, there was typically very little corresponding talk on the significance of investing your time.

Assuming you account for approximately sixteen hours of each day either working or sleeping, **that leaves about eight hours of every day to 'spend or invest' as you choose.** This will ultimately play a major part in defining your life.

Keep the main thing, the main thing.

When you decide to invest and not spend the lion-share of these "eight-great hours" to sketch out and follow a detailed blueprint to achieve meaningful personal and professional goals, you will discover a new path filled with daily experiences that are exciting and rewarding.

There is a great sense of control when you are managing your schedule instead of it managing you. You transform from being preyed upon by an overwhelming amount of requests for your time and attention, to a person who confidently sets boundaries aligning time investments with your values, priorities, and goals.

This time investment makeover will also lift and strengthen your spirit. Establishing a new tone and tempo for your life will eliminate the flashes of anger you feel towards yourself and others. This includes the subsequent repercussions of shame and guilt that occur for those living a reactive, and not proactive, life.

A daily schedule that is investment-based allows you to get more of the right things done. Instead of shutting down due to overload, or working non-stop in a desperate attempt to dig out, you will now be following a realistic path to progress.

And like all good investment strategies, the rewards have an enriching compound effect.

You will experience a greater sense of calm and peace of mind from the comfort of knowing that you are doing the right thing at the right time and that you are following a plan that will allow you to get the important activities done.

Translate your priorities into actions.

Now an earnest effort to planning your day can give you clarity on your priorities and increase your sense of mental order and control. But it cannot guarantee everything will go perfectly and prevent people from making requests for a piece of your precious day. The key to becoming an intelligent investor of time is you must zealously **put your proactive goals ahead of your reactive tasks.**

Create a Base Schedule
Start with a blank weekly calendar, and then block in all of your "fixed time costs" (i.e., work, sleep, fitness, relationships, spiritual, etc.) You must protect time for the activities related to your most vital priorities. Establish routines for recurring time costs (i.e., how much sleep do you need to be most effective? What time do you need to wake up to be at work on time? Do you choose to pray and/or exercise every day? Etc.)

Use the "INO" Technique
The pursuit of excellence is laudable when you are working on your most important projects, but this high standard will prove to be detrimental with lesser tasks. Using the "INO" Technique - Investment, Neutral and Optimize - will maximize your time ROI by categorizing activities (professionally and personally),

and help you decide the amount of time and energy to devote to each.

Categories include the:

- **Investment Category**: This holds activities that could lead to a significant increase in benefits you receive (i.e., career-enhancing projects; quality time on important relationships.)
- **Neutral Category**: Shows activities that give back as much as you put into them (i.e., hourly work; pleasure reading.)
- **Optimize Category:** Features activities that the more time spent on them, the benefits decrease (i.e., routine email or paperwork; cleaning the house.)

At the start of each day, you can label each activity with an **"I,"** **"N," or "O"** to help you remember whether it's worth putting more time and energy into it.

Leverage Technology

Harness the power of mobile and web-based apps to boost your scheduling efficiency. Consider adding one or more of these tools to your planning arsenal: Todoist; Evernote; Wunderlist; TeuxDeux; or Remember the Milk. The person you are today is the sum total of how you have spent your time to date. When you shift to consistently investing your time in specific, prioritized activities, you will begin the transformation to becoming the person you want to be.

About Elizabeth Grace Saunders

Elizabeth Grace Saunders is the founder and CEO of Real Life E -- a time coaching company that empowers individuals who feel guilty, overwhelmed and frustrated to feel peaceful, confident and accomplished.

She was named one of the World's Top 30 Time Management Professionals. Real Life E offers both one-on-one time management coaching as well as a Time Management Made Easy group coaching program. The Christian division of her company focuses on a faith-based approach to time management through Divine Time Management Group Coaching.

McGraw Hill published her first book, *The 3 Secrets to Effective Time Investment: How to Achieve More Success with Less Stress.* Harvard Business Review published her second book, *How to Invest Your Time Like Money.* FaithWords published her third book, *Divine Time Management.* Elizabeth contributes to blogs like Harvard Business Review and Fast Company and has appeared on CBS, ABC, NBC, and Fox.

Elizabeth's Recommendations

Read One Book
The 3 Secrets To Time Investment: How To Achieve More Success With Less Stress by Elizabeth Grace Saunders.
This book addresses the three key elements of effective time investment: priorities, expectations, and routines.

Visit One Website
HBR.org
A great source of educational content for the best in management thinking.

Subscribe to One Podcast
HurrySlowly.co   (.co not .com)
This Podcast shows how you can be more productive, creative, and resilient through the simple act of slowing down.

31

"Deliver experiences that put smiles on your customers' faces."

Jim Baugh
Founder
PHIT America

Former President
Wilson Sporting Goods

It has been stated by many people who had the pleasure of working with and for Mr. Walt Disney that he was a master of the philosophy of keeping things simple so that everyone understood the message.

One of the most enduring leadership lessons that has been passed down in the Disney enterprise and continues to define their customer experience strategy are **Walt's wise words:**

"You don't build it for yourself. You know what the people want, and you build it for them."

Our role as business leaders and sales professionals is to, 'know what the people want' and provide products and services that make the lives of people easier and more enjoyable.

Putting smiles on customers' faces is where your business will also find its happiness.

Research strongly indicates that companies who successfully implement a customer experience strategy will earn higher customer satisfaction ratings, will reduce their customer turnover and will increase revenues.

According to the Digital Marketing Trends Report conducted by Econsultancy and Adobe, it was found that companies view improving customer experiences as the best opportunity for their organization to grow their business. Research by Gartner Inc. supports this position, stating that **81% of companies polled expected to compete mostly or completely on the basis of customer experience in 2019.**

A wise strategy, as a study by American Express found that 60% of customers are willing to pay more for a better experience. And a complementary analysis performed by Oracle revealed that 74% of senior executives believe that customer experience impacts the willingness of a customer to be a loyal supporter of the brand.

And it's important to note that a great customer experience means going beyond delivering excellent customer service. Interacting with a customer, whether in person or on the phone and meeting their needs, is indeed a critical component. But offering an option that includes unexpected perks (i.e., better pricing; better terms; faster delivery, etc.) creates a very memorable experience.

However, there is evidence of a significant disconnect between what companies believe they are delivering in the area of customer experience and the customer's perception of what must be remedied.

According to research by Bain and Company revealed that 80% of the companies analyzed believed their customer experience was great, while shockingly, only 8% of their customers agreed with them.

The answers to aligning your well-intended efforts to produce image of difference customer experiences with improved tangible results can be found in these tactical changes:

Clarify Your Identity and Strategy
Restate internally the company's vision of what your brand strives to deliver to each and every customer. Then set a new integrated course of action to implement and track the results.

Give Customers More Self Service
Customers want the ability to be proactive and solve their own problems and expect a robust company website with a very user-friendly self-service application.

Capture Customer Feedback
This can be an outbound follow up call by a customer service agent or a post-interaction email survey that will gather the data of the customer's opinion of the completed transaction.

Get Your Feet Dirty

If you are in a sales leadership position, it is imperative that you get out from behind your desk and get in the field. Face to face meetings keep you connected to the people who are on the front lines dealing with the customers buying your product.

Manage Pricing and Products for All Providers

Work diligently to maintain a pricing structure and product offerings that will keep small but essential accounts viable and in the game. Major retailers undoubtedly drive the numbers, but local grass root influencers have a valued place in the market.

Focus on delivering experiences that put smiles on customers' faces and you will build your own magic kingdom that customers will flock to and never want to leave!

About Jim Baugh

A successful pioneer and leader of the sports & fitness industry and physical activity advocate.

Jim's background is filled with leadership positions while pioneering new technologies implementing people-oriented marketing approaches which are geared to put smiles on people's faces. He has been President of Wilson Sporting Goods, General Manager of the Tennis Division & Golf Division at Wilson and was VP of Sales & Marketing at Prince. He revolutionized tennis multiple times with the rollout of the oversized Prince racquet, the widebody Wilson Profile racquet & superlight Hammer racquets which lead Wilson to a 54% market share. He also launched state of the art introductions in golf and tennis footwear. Jim always used a grassroots approach focusing on 'game improvement products for the average player.'

He also led 'movements' to grow industries, participation and improve the health of Americans. He united the tennis industry to grow participation by 7 million players in 6 years. He developed new ways for people to learn to play tennis with Tennis Welcome Centers and Cardio Tennis. Jim then rebuilt the 'roots' of physical activity by rebuilding physical education programs when he founded PE4life almost 20 years ago and, most recently, with PHIT America, his second national charity. PHIT America is fighting the 'Inactivity Pandemic' with expanded school PE programs.
PHIT America has helped over 300,000 children in over 600 schools nationwide get physically active.

With all of this, Jim has been inducted into the Sports Industry Hall of Fame and Tennis Industry Hall of Fame. He also awarded from Rider University the *"Distinguished Alumnus Award"* given to those who have achieved *exceptional attainment in life.*

Jim's Recommendations

Read One Book
The Power of Moments: Why Certain Experiences Have Extraordinary Impact by Chip Heath & Dan Heath
The New York Times bestselling authors of *Switch* and *Made to Stick* explore why certain brief experiences can jolt us and elevate us and change us—and how we can learn to create such extraordinary moments in our life and work.

Visit One Website
PHITAmerica.org
Promoting the movement for a Fit and Healthy America.

Subscribe to One Podcast
Big Life Kids (Search on Stitcher.com)
This popular podcast teaches children to stay resilient, believe in themselves, and face life's challenges with confidence.

32

"Immerse customers in an AFTER-world experience."

Stuart Paap
Founder
Pitch DNA

At the end of World War I there was a popular song titled, *"How Ya Gonna Keep Them Down On The Farm (After They've Seen Paree?)* and the lyrics raised the amusing question about the problem of getting soldiers from rural environments to return to their mundane farm work after experiencing European city life and the exhilarating culture of Paris.

Yes, the power of experiencing something for yourself, rather than being shown or told about it is the timeless, and extremely successful, art of seduction that needs to be quickly and efficiently incorporated into every encounter with a prospective customer.

Being properly prepared and buttoned down with product knowledge are essential elements for closing any deal, but the key ingredient to winning the day is the practice of giving the customer the experience of their life AFTER using your product or service.

Give people a taste of the AFTER-world.

As a species, we are by nature very complacent, and we don't realize how much we have benefitted from products and services AFTER the fact. We forget, or perhaps never knew, about how things were done BEFORE with the use of camcorders, cameras and pay phones AFTER we have experienced the magic of smartphones.

So view each setting as being in the BEFORE phase and you have to transport your users to the AFTER phase, as often and as quickly as you can. You want to create a cognitive dissonance – a bit of an empty feeling – of what it is like to not have what you are offering.

Embracing this energizing exercise of elevating experiencing above explaining will give a high percentage of prospects the distinct feeling of added value and a better way to proceed.

Every person (customer) is playing the hero in their own life movie.

When you consider the obvious that we all want to be seen in the best light possible by those viewing our work, it is easier to focus on the aspects of your product that will make the client's job easier, and them more efficient and successful.

You want people to experience the **AFTER** world of life connected to your product or service.

Research, and likely personal observation, indicate that customers want to remain loyal to their suppliers – few people enjoy shopping and rethinking their vendor list – but you must continue to reinforce this customer mindset.

We don't see things as **they** are.
We see things as **we** are.

So make the decision easy for a new prospect to come into the fold, by implementing the following action steps:

Who, What, and How
Clarify who the decision-makers are and who the intended audience is for your presentation. Confirm the subject you are covering and be crystal clear on the objectives that need to be addressed and solved. And carve your presentation down to three to five key points and deliver your message vividly, but succinctly.

Add Value To The Valuables

Commit to being an agent of change by adding extreme value to the universal priorities of time, energy and money. Your presentation must offer product experiences that will demonstrate the client's workday will be more productive, more efficient and less costly, or they are of no benefit to the customer.

Feedback Keeps You On Track

Validate what you believe you are seeing and hearing by gathering feedback right on the spot or with a follow-up survey via email or phone call.

Pay Attention Details

Vacuum up every bit of data offered up before, during and after the presentation. New information acted on before a final decision is made could be the missing piece that pivots the outcome in your favor.

So unchain your creative spirit and get your product or service into the hands and minds of the targeted user by painting an irresistible 'big city' experience that will make it impossible for the customer or prospect to consider returning to the farm!

About Stuart Paap

Stuart helps startups, entrepreneurs, and business leaders perfect their pitches, presentations, and speeches. He regularly leads workshops for universities, incubators, and tech companies, including MassChallenge, the MIT Enterprise Forum, McGill's X-1 Accelerator, Northeastern's RISE, the Brandeis SPARK Program, the Tufts 100K New Ventures Competition, and more.

Stuart has been featured in the Boston Sunday Globe, U.S. New and World Report and Creator Magazine.

He writes a monthly column on effective communication for his subscribers at PitchDNA.com.

You can also find on Twitter @stuartpitch and Instagram @pitchdna.

Stuart's Recommendations

Read One Book
To Sell Is Human by Daniel H. Pink
This book explores the surprising truth about moving others.

Visit One Website
Bakadesuyo.com by Eric Barker
It's all about barking up the wrong tree.

Subscribe to One Podcast
The Knowledge Project Podcast with Shane Parrish
This podcast helps you master the best of what other people have already figured out.

33

"Bring your best self, every day."

Adnan Chaudhry
Senior Vice President, Commercial Sales
Salesforce

The noted theologian and Trappist monk Thomas Merton, stated that happiness is not a matter of intensity but of balance, order, rhythm, and harmony.

Now the good news is you do not need to live a monk's existence of simplicity and separateness to achieve your goals of a fulfilling and rewarding personal and professional life.

The challenge is to sustain a commitment to excellence in both areas by focusing on your whole self. As high performance psychologist Michael Gervais believes; this begins with a concentrated effort on the areas you can control - your mind, your body, and your craft.

Give yourself permission to start over, every day.

To unlock your full potential and maximize your time and talent at home and at work you must take complete ownership of your life. Any comfort derived from misplaced energy spent blaming other people or circumstances for your failings or situation will now be funneled to strengthening your mental and physical well-being.

It starts with training your mind. View your happiness and peace of mind as a skill or muscle that can be developed and strengthened. Making a conscious and consistent effort to have a positive mindset and an attitude of gratitude will be the foundation that everything you say, do, and accomplish is built on.

Being consistent with your efforts literally rewires your brain.

According to Swedish psychologist, K. Anders Ericsson, anytime we perform a task consistently we start to experience a process called, Myelination. This process forms very thin (myelin) sheaths around our nerves that allow impulses to move more quickly. This demonstrates how the brain adapts to various challenges by rewiring itself in ways that increase its ability to carry out the functions required.

So consider reaping the mental rewards of a consistent routine that begins each day when you wake up. Start with a couple deep nourishing breaths; forming one mental image of gratitude and a single intention for the day. Follow this with five minutes of calming meditation better known nowadays as "mindfulness." Just by simply pressing the reset button in the mind, it stimulates powerful changes in our brains to facilitate a fresh start of the day.

Shifting focus to your body, remember that, *'the day begins the night before'* and sleep is the most significant performance enhancer available to us.

Turn off all electronic devices one hour before bedtime.

To maximize your slumber, try using a traditional alarm clock. If you prefer to have your phone serve as an alarm, put it into "airplane mode" which limits interruptions (and alerts) to only the alarm and nothing else. Texts and emails should not be the last thing going through your mind -- or the first thing you see when in bed.

If you are operating on less than eight hours of sleep a night, the research will show that you are both physically and cognitively impaired. The cumulative effect of this detrimental routine will manifest itself in a compromised immune system and make you increasingly susceptible to illness.

Consistent diet and exercise are the other two critical components for transforming your body into a fine-tuned machine.

There is no shortage of healthy eating programs to consider, but one that calls for consuming less processed food offerings is an excellent place to start. And many who are committed to an exercise regimen of some cardio and stretching enjoy beginning their day with it, but midday or evening may fit your schedule and temperament better.

Start your day with a win.

With a mind that is grateful and positive, and a body that is rested and ready, you will be firing on all cylinders to pursue with vigor your personal and professional goals.

Diving in with enthusiasm will stoke your passion and steadily raise your level of proficiency in every endeavor on your radar.

And adding these three tactics into your daily body of work will inevitably lift your profile and provide more opportunities for personal growth and professional success in your chosen craft:

Bring Intellectual Curiosity

Be intellectually inquisitive about everything related to your customer's success. Understanding customer issues as well as they do will give you a greater chance to be their 'go-to' problem solver.

Sharpen Your Business Acumen

Research and document your customer's strategic goals, initiatives, and challenges to enhance your knowledge of how their business runs. This will help address the customer's problem with a viable commercial solution.

Got Grit?

Professionals who have demonstrated unwavering stamina and sticktoitiveness in their life experiences are always in demand.

So be consistent in your efforts to sharpen your mind and strengthen your body, and you will enjoy the personal and professional happiness that comes with living a balanced life!

About Adnan Chaudhry

Adnan Chaudhry is Senior Vice President, Commercial Sales at Salesforce.com focusing on the coverage of strategic accounts in the U.S. He has also held sales leadership roles within the Financial Services vertical at Salesforce.

Prior to returning to Salesforce, Adnan was Group Vice President, Global Sales at Oracle where he led the global sales organization for the Utilities and Energy vertical. Adnan joined Oracle in May 2016 through its acquisition of Opower (NYSE:OPWR), which is the leader in cloud-based energy information software and services to the utility sector. While at Opower, he was Senior Vice President, Sales and part of the executive team taking the company from approx. $25 mil to $155 mil in revenue over four years, and through its April 2014 IPO and subsequent acquisition by Oracle.

Previously, Adnan was an associate at private-equity firm Hicks, Muse, Tate & Furst, focusing on managing the firm's consumer and media investment portfolio. He later served as Vice President of Corporate Development and Strategic Planning at Swift & Company, a portfolio company of Hicks Muse. Adnan began his career as an investment-banking analyst at Salomon Smith Barney in New York.

Adnan graduated from the University of Utah with a BS in Finance and a BA in Economics and received an MBA from the Stanford Graduate School of Business.

Adnan's Recommendations

Read One Book
Why We Sleep by Matthew Walker
This New York Times bestselling book explains how a good night's sleep can make us, 'cleverer, more attractive, slimmer, happier, healthier, and ward off cancer.'

Visit One Website
Salesforce.com
Salesforce is a cloud-based software company headquartered in San Francisco that was ranked first in Fortune's 100 Best Companies to Work for in 2018.

Subscribe to One Podcast
Finding Mastery by Michael Gervais
Dr. Michael Gervais is fascinated by the psychology of high performance and is excited to share the many paths towards, Finding Mastery.

Join the
'One Thing'
Conversation

OneThingTheBook.com

Connect with our thought leaders and
all the resources mentioned inside.

*For Bulk and Corporate Orders please
inquire by visiting the website above.*

Other Works by
Tim Malloy and Billy Martin

60 Seconds on Officiating
Ref60.com

The Zebra Foundation
ProjectZebra.org

Officiating Publications

Beyond the Rules
Volume I and Volume II

The Best of
"60 Seconds on Officiating"

Game Tracker
Journal

2019 Bluebook 60 (14th Edition)
"The Ultimate Guide to Fastpitch Softball Rules"
BlueBook60.com

bit.ly/AuthorBillyMartin
Short Link to Billy's Author Page on Amazon

(link is case sensitive)

More Leadership Resources

Are you ready to …
"Live the Coaching Culture?"

The benefits are obvious and important. In today's high pressure sales organizations the ability to recruit, hire, train, and retain top talent is critical for a company's success. Possessing solid coaching skills is the key to support these initiatives.

The *FLIP'D Coaching for Sales Performance*™ workshop leverages industry leading practices and coaching models to provide an easy-to-consume and easy-to-implement sales coaching framework.

Layer on some practical tools with expert coaching, including co-facilitation using individuals from your organization, and this creates an amazing single day workshop experience.

For more information visit:

FLIPDCoaching.com

cco@flipdcoaching.com
Chief Coaching Officer (Email)

Home of the *"FLIP'D Around"* Leadership Blog

Made in the USA
Middletown, DE
21 August 2019